# ONE BEST HIKE
# MOUNT WHITN

# ONE BEST HIKE: MOUNT WHITNEY

### Everything you need to know to successfully hike California's highest peak

SECOND EDITION

## Elizabeth Wenk

WILDERNESS PRESS ... *on the trail since 1967*

**One Best Hike: Mount Whitney**

Published by Wilderness Press
Distributed by Publishers Group West
Printed in the United States of America
Second edition, first printing

Cover and interior photos copyright © 2017 by Elizabeth Wenk
Cover design: Larry B. Van Dyke
Book design: Andreas Schueller and Larry B. Van Dyke
Maps: Elizabeth Wenk

Library of Congress Cataloging-in-Publication Data

Names: Wenk, Elizabeth, author.
Title: One best hike : Mount Whitney : everything you need to know to
    successfully hike California's highest peak / Elizabeth Wenk.
Description: Birmingham, AL : Wilderness Press, [2016] | Series: One Best Hike |
    "Distributed by Publishers Group West"T.p. verso. | Includes index.
Identifiers: LCCN 2016018250 (print) | LCCN 2016033877 (ebook) | ISBN
    9780899978321 (paperback) | ISBN 9780899978338 (ebook | ISBN
    9780899979304 (hardcover)
Subjects: LCSH: Mountaineering—California—Whitney, Mount—Guidebooks. |
    Hiking—California—Whitney, Mount—Guidebooks. | Backpacking—California
    —Whitney, Mount—Guidebooks. | Whitney, Mount (Calif.)—Guidebooks.
Classification: LCC GV199.42.C22 W44 2016 (print) | LCC GV199.42.C22 (ebook)
    | DDC 796.55209794/86—dc23
LC record available at https://lccn.loc.gov/2016018250

🐾 **WILDERNESS PRESS**
    An imprint of AdventureKEEN
    2204 First Ave. S, Ste. 102
    Birmingham, AL 35233

Visit wildernesspress.com for a complete listing of our books and for ordering information. Contact us at our website, at facebook.com/wildernesspress1967, or at twitter
.com/wilderness1967 with questions or comments. To find out more about who we are
and what we're doing, visit blog.wildernesspress.com.

*Front cover, top to bottom:* Trailside Meadow; descending to Whitney Portal; sunrise
on the Whitney skyline as seen from Trail Camp
*Back cover, top to bottom:* Between Outpost Camp and Mirror Lake; Trail Camp
*Frontispiece:* View to Lone Pine Peak, Wotans Throne, and Consultation Lake

**SAFETY NOTICE:** Although Wilderness Press and the author have made every
attempt to ensure that the information in this book is accurate at press time, they are
not responsible for any loss, damage, injury, or inconvenience that may occur to any-
one while using this book. You are responsible for your own safety and health while
in the wilderness. The fact that a trail is described in this book does not mean that it
will be safe for you. Be aware that trail conditions can change from day to day. Always
check local conditions and know your own limitations.

# Acknowledgments

I dedicate this book to all who have showed me the many ways that mountains, especially those in the Sierra Nevada, can be endlessly captivating and enchanting.

Foremost, I thank my husband and two daughters for their support when I wrote both the original book and the current revision. I have slowly discovered that writing books is a job never finished, as I am forever thinking about what to change and wondering how I should look at a trail the next time I walk it. My family good-humoredly joins me on many hikes and listens to my incessant ponderings.

Carolyn Tiernan, MD, reviewed all medical sections for the first edition, providing important feedback. Inga Aksamit and Kenny Meyer, the moderators for the Altitude Acclimatization Facebook group, reviewed the text on altitude sickness for this edition.

Hal Klieforth commented on the text on Sierra weather and human history for the first edition and provided me unlimited access to his extensive library of Sierra literature. He has since passed, and I enormously miss his enthusiasm and support as I work on books. Steve Cosner, the moderator for the Whitney Zone forum, provided extensive comments on the entire manuscript—these were incredibly valuable.

I add my appreciation to Wilderness Press for providing me the opportunity to write this book. They allowed me the freedom to express my approach to hiking: that you need to look at and think about natural history and human history as you follow the trail upward.

—*Lizzy Wenk*

# Mount Whitney Locator Map

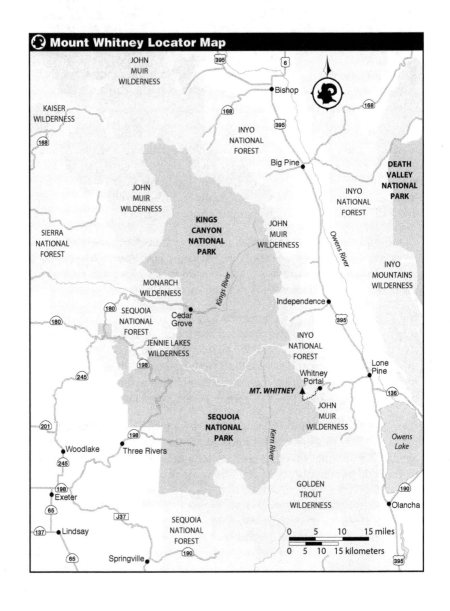

# Contents

## 1

# Introduction

*Whitney is easily accessible to all whose heart and lungs can stand its rarified atmosphere, and probably no other mountain in the world unascended by a railway can boast such an enrollment of visitors.*

**—Marion Parsons,**
the first woman to serve on the Sierra Club
board of directors and a member of a
1909 Sierra Club ascent of Mount Whitney

## Mount Whitney and the Mount Whitney Trail

The summit of Mount Whitney has been a sought-after destination since 1864, when the peak was first surveyed as the highest in the United States. Although the number of ascents per year has risen hundredfold since Marion Parsons's time, her sentiments still ring true today. One of the most iconic peaks in the country, 14,505-foot Whitney stands 72 feet higher than Colorado's Mount Elbert, making it the highest peak in the contiguous 48 states (Alaska's 20,320-foot Denali is the highest in the United States).

The steep, eastern face of Mount Whitney is exquisite—the last in a dramatic series of jagged peaks, nearly each one higher than the previous, culminating in the summit of Mount Whitney. This vista is powerful from the peak's base town of Lone Pine, more than 10,000 feet below in the Owens Valley.

*Opposite and above:* Looking east to Lone Pine Lake with the Inyo Mountains behind

Mount Whitney's top is a desired destination for reasons other than its lofty elevation: it's a beautiful peak, in easy driving reach of 30 million people, and, perhaps most important, the summit is not a giveaway. Whitney is tough enough to give you a real challenge, but not so tough that you need technical mountaineering equipment and a guide. Indeed, the 20.8-mile trail (up and back) is a distance that most people can hike with appropriate training and planning.

The Mount Whitney Trail is what makes the summit an achievable goal. Before the trail was built in 1904, it was impossible to summit in a day or even a long weekend, as Hubert Dyer, an early Sierra mountaineer and a charter member of the Sierra Club, reported in 1893:

> *To one standing near these structures the stupendous mass of the Sierras seems hanging over them and the summit of Whitney but a little way off. Yet it is about seventy miles by the shortest trail to the summit. There are stories told of men who have climbed the great eastern face. Though possible, it is a dangerous undertaking.*

Today, about 10,000 people each year successfully summit Mount Whitney by the well-maintained Mount Whitney Trail, the easiest route up that great eastern face. There's no reason why you can't be one of them.

The goals of this book are threefold. First, it aims to provide novice hikers and hikers new to the high-elevation Sierra Nevada with the background information to safely summit Mount Whitney—or to know when conditions such as health or weather mean that it's time to turn around and make another summit bid in the future. It is also meant to provide the information all hikers need to plan a summit bid: details on wilderness permits, what to eat, and where to sleep in Lone Pine; what gear is essential; and, of course, everything you need to know about hiking up the Mount Whitney Trail itself. This book will also give you a better understanding of the human and natural history of the Mount Whitney area.

Many people, especially day hikers, will rightfully question the notion of carrying a guidebook to the summit of the peak. When will you have time to admire plants or geologic features on the ascent? My advice is to read the chapters "Precautions and Considerations" (page 31) and "Preparations and Planning" (page 57) before your hike. Then photocopy the route description, elevation profile, sketch map of the route, and labeled panorama from the summit (pages 136–137) to carry with you. The rest of the book can be a souvenir of a wonderful hike, and you can read the background information at your leisure. If you are backpacking and can take a more unhurried pace, consider carrying the entire book up (it is, after all, less than 7 ounces). You might find yourself looking at the plants and geologic features along the trail and be pleased to learn more about them. Or, as you eat a snack, you can read a little about the history of Mount Whitney. Regardless of how you do it, you're sure to fall in love with this iconic peak.

# Human History

As a mountaineering destination, a survey point, a scientific laboratory, or simply the backdrop for Western films, Mount Whitney has long captured people's interest.

### EARLY VIEWS OF MOUNT WHITNEY

The first white men to see Mount Whitney were probably members of a party led by Western explorer Joseph Walker in 1834. They traveled south from the Truckee River, passing through the Owens Valley before crossing to the western side of the Sierra Nevada at Walker Pass. However, these men were not surveyors and did not know which of the many peaks along the escarpment was the highest, much less that one peak would have the distinction of being taller than the already well-known Cascade volcanoes.

Over the next three decades, as various mining booms occurred, ever more people moved to the Owens Valley and the surrounding mountains, but most did not venture deep into the Sierra. It was only on July 2, 1864, when Mount Whitney was first viewed and surveyed from the west, that it achieved its status as the highest in the country. On that day, William Brewer and Charles Hoffmann, respectively a botanist (and field crew leader) and a topographer for the California State Geological Survey, made the first ascent of 13,570-foot Mount Brewer and saw the layout of the southern High Sierra for the first time, including the location of the tallest peak in the range. (Whitney relinquished its title of "tallest in the US" in 1959, when Alaska, with its 20,320-foot Denali and 15 other peaks taller than Mount Whitney, was admitted to the United States.)

*Continued on page 6*

## WHITNEY'S "CHANGING" ELEVATION

"Few mountain elevations have been discussed more carefully than that of Mt. Whitney," said meteorologist Alexander McAdie in 1904. The debate continues today.

Over the years, more refined techniques and better estimates of other California elevations have led to more accurate measurements for Mount Whitney. Estimates have ranged from 14,423 feet to nearly 15,000 feet, and its altitude is currently listed at 14,505 feet.

In 1864 members of the Whitney Survey made the first estimates of Mount Whitney's elevation from the summits of Mount Brewer and Mount Tyndall. They used handheld compasses to determine Mount Whitney's location through triangulation, and they used the vertical angle between their location and Mount Whitney's summit to determine its elevation. These surveys suggested that the summit stood well above 14,500 feet.

To determine the elevation from the summit itself, the 19th-century surveyors carried mercury barometers. Scientists determined the air pressure, temperature, and vapor pressure and compared these results to others simultaneously obtained at a nearby location whose altitude was known. (Accommodating weather was required for acceptable barometer readings, and these early readings were often erroneous.) In this way, Carl Rabe, a member of the third ascent party, made the first summit measurements on September 6, 1873, and estimated Whitney's elevation at 14,898 feet.

This number was quoted in official sources for several decades, but more accurate estimates were soon available, including the Wheeler Survey's 1875 estimate of 14,471 feet and Samuel Langley's 1881 estimate of 14,522 feet.

A persistent problem with these estimates was the uncertain elevation of Lone Pine, a nearby reference point for Mount Whitney. Langley's 1881 elevation was recalculated to 14,423 feet when a new elevation estimate (based on the railroad grade) for Lone Pine became available.

In 1905, and again in the late 1920s, the elevation of Mount Whitney was determined quite accurately by running leveling

lines from Lone Pine to the summit. During the summers of
1925 and 1928, workers with the U.S. Coast and Geodetic
Survey laboriously laid planks end to end from Lone Pine to
Whitney's summit to determine horizontal distance. After
every few planks, they used a leveling instrument to determine change in elevation, sighting to a 12-foot rod a known
distance away. They then added the many incremental
increases in elevation. Remarkably, the two surveys done in
this way yielded elevations that differed by just 5 feet.

The U.S. Geological Survey (USGS) placed benchmarks on
boulders at the summit of Mount Whitney to indicate these
known elevations. Because of the differing heights of each
boulder, these benchmarks differ by several feet and do not
really represent the height of the mountain. Of the eight
benchmarks on the summit, GT1811, placed in 1950 and
attached directly to bedrock is *the* Mount Whitney bench-
mark, and its height is 14,505 feet. The other benchmarks
range in (current) height from 14,499 to 14,508 feet, with the
higher benchmarks attached to protruding boulders—such as
GT1809, which is near the Mount Whitney plaque.

The benchmarks' elevations have changed with time largely
because *elevation* is a relative term. It implies elevation above
mean sea level, but what exactly is mean sea level (MSL)? In
any given location on Earth, MSL is defined as the average of
high and low tides across a 19-year cycle. But across the globe
MSL differs by hundreds of feet (in comparison to a smooth
ellipsoid) because of differences in the density of the Earth's
crust, which changes the strength of the gravitational pull
toward the center of the Earth. Today, geographic reference
systems use a quasi-elliptical model of the Earth's surface,
termed a geoid, to determine elevation. All points on the
surface of the geoid have the same gravitational potential,
and elevation is defined as the distance above this surface.
Because the mass of the inside of the Earth is not uniform, the
calculated geoids are remarkably bumpy—they cannot be
defined by a simple mathematical equation.

*(Continued on page 6)*

*(Continued from page 5)*

The change in reference elevations is responsible for the 1988 change in Mount Whitney's "official" elevation from 14,497 to 14,505 feet. Although the geoid continues to be refined, North American Vertical Datum of 1988 (NAVD88) remains quite accurate for the Sierra. (Note that most printed USGS maps still use the National Geodetic Vertical Datum of 1929 [NGVD29] and therefore indicate different elevations from those calculated by the more recent survey.)

An added confusion is that the frame of reference used by GPS units is the World Geodetic System 1984 (WGS84), which estimates elevation based on a simple ellipsoid. In some locations these elevations are hundreds of feet different from the geoid-based elevations. Fortunately on Mount Whitney, the altitude displayed on an uncorrected GPS unit will only be a 3.9-foot underestimate of the geoid-based elevation. Also, note that WGS84 defines both vertical and horizontal coordinates. Some of the other reference standards provide only vertical (for example, NAVD88, NGVD29, GRS80) or horizontal (for example, NAD27, NAD83) datum. The horizontal datums adjust the X-Y coordinates that define your location, while the vertical datums adjust your elevation.

Finally, because plate tectonics are probably continuing to push Mount Whitney slowly skyward, erosive forces are grinding it downward, and geographers continue to refine the shape of their ellipsoid model, the elevation of Whitney is likely to change again.

*Continued from page 3*

## RACE FOR FIRST ASCENT

The race to ascend the high point began two days later. Two other members of the geological survey, Clarence King, a geologist and daredevilish explorer, and Dick Cotter, an assistant, begged permission to head to the peak. They went through uncharted country: across the Kings-Kern Divide and into the Kern River drainage. Thinking they were heading for the Sierra Nevada's high point, they ascended along a fork of Tyndall Creek and summited not Whitney but 14,019-foot Mount Tyndall, the Sierra's eighth-highest peak.

From the top, they surveyed the surrounding peaks, noting several that were higher, including Mount Whitney. Upon their ascent, King named Mount Tyndall after a famous British scientist and Mount Whitney after the chief of the California State Geological Survey.

The desire to be the first to summit Mount Whitney had seized King. On a resupply stop in Visalia, he begged to detour back to the Whitney region for another attempt. He received permission to temporarily leave the party for a second attempt to reach Mount Whitney. With two cavalrymen and a few horses, he again set out for the Kern River drainage, this time via the Hockett Trail from the San Joaquin Valley. En route, he passed today's Mount Langley, calling it Sheep Mountain, and continued to Mount Whitney. He made it within about 300 feet of the summit.

In 1871 King made a third attempt, this time from the Owens Valley, via a southern route. In writing about the stormy day when he ascended the "true" summit of Mount Whitney, King noted that he thought he saw Mount Tyndall some distance to the north. But two years later, a family from Lone Pine climbed Sheep Mountain, found King's summit note, and informed him that he had stood on a summit some miles south of Mount Whitney.

It wasn't entirely King's fault because, on his map, the name Mount Whitney was mistakenly attached to Mount Langley. In 1870 Charles Hoffmann led a survey to the Inyo Mountains, and maps created after the survey erroneously indicated that Mount Langley was Mount Whitney. Ironically, the error was in part due to King, who made faulty compass measurements from the summit of Mount Tyndall in 1864. Moreover, Langley and Whitney have similar shapes, and from lower elevations, such as the location of Hoffmann's survey team, it is difficult to distinguish which peak is higher. Two meadows on the Kern Plateau to the west of Mount Langley are a relic of this mapping mistake, as they still hold the name Whitney.

By the 1870s people from Lone Pine were regularly crossing into the Kern drainage to escape the Owens Valley summers. They took the Hockett Trail from its eastern terminus in Lone Pine, climbed to Horseshoe Meadows, crossed the Sierra Crest at Cottonwood Pass, and then traversed the Kern Plateau before dropping to the Kern River near today's Kern River ranger station, at the southern boundary of Sequoia National Park. In 1873 three men, Charles D. Begole, Albert H. Johnson, and John Lucas, who were camped along the Kern River, decided to leave their fishing camp for a few days and head toward the Sierra Crest. On their trip, they summited first Mount Langley and then, on August 18, 1873, from the southwest, made the first ascent of Mount Whitney. They left the Hockett Trail and traveled north, probably passing the vicinity of Crabtree Meadow, before climbing east toward Mount Whitney. In subsequent weeks, two more parties successfully climbed Whitney: William Crapo and Abe Leyda in late August, and William Crapo, William L. Hunter, Tom McDonough, and Carl Rabe on September 6, 1873. (The men in the second and third ascent parties attacked the claims made by the three fishermen, but the fishermen's truthful story eventually prevailed.)

Meanwhile, upon hearing that he had ascended the wrong peak in 1871, Clarence King left his survey job on the East Coast and rushed back to California to attempt Whitney again. On September 19, 1873, King finally succeeded, along with partner Frank Knowles, but they had to settle for fourth place.

## OTHER EARLY ASCENTS

On October 21, 1873, naturalist John Muir pioneered a new route from the east that is now known as the Mountaineers Route. However, for many years, the nontechnical route up the western face remained the most popular. Indeed, once the early summiteers showed that it was fairly easy to climb Mount Whitney from the west, it quickly became a sought-after climb. Parties continued to follow the Hockett Trail across the Sierra Crest and then traveled north via the Kern Plateau, Rock Creek, and Guyot Pass to reach Crabtree Meadow. Some parties would reach the summit in a long day from Crabtree Meadow, but most established a higher camp near Guitar Lake. It was via this route that, in the summer of 1878, the first woman, Anna Mills, climbed to the summit.

In 1896 A. W. de la Cour Carroll, a charter member of the Sierra Club from Lone Pine, was the first to describe an ascent via a route similar to today's Mount Whitney Trail. His party of five men and three women left the vicinity of Outpost Camp early on August 28, 1895, and followed Lone Pine Creek up to Consultation Lake. It appears that from there they climbed toward Whitney Pass (nearly a mile southeast of Trail Crest). From there, they descended toward Hitchcock and Guitar Lakes, where they spent a night before climbing the mountain. This circuitous route took them down 2,500 feet and then immediately back up again to avoid a traverse of the pinnacles south of Mount Whitney's summit. Luckily, on the return,

## NAMING OF WHITNEY

Like many great peaks, Mount Whitney has had a variety of names and much controversy over its official name. The Paiute Indians who inhabited the Owens Valley knew the mountain as Too-man-i-goo-yah, which translates to "very old man." In 1864 the Whitney Survey named the summit Mount Whitney, to honor Josiah Dwight Whitney, the chief of the California State Geological Survey. However, in 1873 the party that claimed the first ascent—three fishermen from Lone Pine, Charles Begole, Albert Johnson, and John Lucas—named the peak Fisherman's Peak to memorialize the first ascent of such a significant peak by three "lowly" fishermen.

In fact, any alternative to Mount Whitney was popular among the Lone Pine locals, who were not fond of the mountain's namesake. Trying to pick a less controversial name, Lone Pine's residents temporarily attached the name Dome of Inyo to the peak but then reverted to Fisherman's Peak. In 1881 a bill was introduced to the California legislature to make Fisherman's Peak the official name. It might have been approved, but as an April 1 prank, a legislator changed the proposed name from Fisherman's Peak to Fowler's Peak. As a result, the governor viewed the entire campaign as a farce and vetoed the bill. And so, Mount Whitney remains the official name.

Carroll identified a passable route closer to Trail Crest, shaving time and distance from their descent. Although others took advantage of this route in the following years, most hikers continued to eschew the steep talus chutes up the east face and instead journeyed over Cottonwood Pass. Indeed, in 1903 a Sierra Club party of 103 ascended from Crabtree Meadow.

## THE MOUNT WHITNEY TRAIL

The initial work on a trail up the eastern slope of Mount Whitney was undertaken during the summer of 1903 by cavalry soldiers. An increase in mountain visitation and interest in climbing Mount Whitney put pressure on the cavalry—at the time charged with protecting the park—to improve visitor services, including building a trail to the summit passable by pack stock. Some funding came from the government, but Lone Pine residents also contributed funding. Lone Pine resident Gustave Marsh wrote letters to his friend, meteorologist Alexander McAdie, that were published in the *Sierra Club Bulletin,* undoubtedly as much to elicit money from its members as to report on progress.

The trail built followed a course similar to the route that A. W. de la Cour Carroll had pioneered nearly a decade earlier. The men

## ASTRONOMY ATOP MOUNT WHITNEY

The large number of peaks named for prominent astronomers (see "Namesakes of Whitney-Area Peaks" on pages 138–139) shows that astronomy and atmospheric research have had a long history in the Mount Whitney area. Astronomers require a high-elevation location, with its thinner atmosphere, and the region is ideal: with its relatively stable weather, measurements can be made on most days.

Samuel Langley, director of the Allegheny Observatory in Pennsylvania, was the first to take advantage of this. In 1881 he measured solar radiation at 11,625 feet, near Guitar Lake, which came to be known as Langley's Camp. His assistant James Keeler repeated some of the measurements on the summit of Mount Whitney. This data allowed Langley to calculate the solar constant, the amount of solar radiation that would reach Earth's surface in the absence of the atmosphere. Although his calculations were significantly higher than the correct number, they were the first estimates of this value, and in 1947 the unit known as the langley was designated as the international unit of solar radiation.

Alexander McAdie, chief forecaster at the San Francisco office of the U.S. Weather Bureau and vice president of the Sierra Club from 1904 to 1913, became a vocal advocate of Mount Whitney as an ideal location for a meteorological observatory following a visit to the summit in 1903. Langley's measurements and McAdie's advertisements led W. Wallace Campbell, longtime director of the Lick Observatory and later president of the University of California, to consider Mount Whitney's summit for his research. He decided it was the perfect place from which to determine if the atmosphere on Mars contained water vapor. These measurements had to be made at a location with little water vapor, and because water vapor decreases more rapidly than oxygen with increased elevation, toiled to build a route through the field of talus, where moving one boulder often initiated an avalanche of rock that damaged the trail downslope. When they reached Whitney Pass (just north of Mount McAdie, nearly a mile southeast of today's Trail Crest), they ran out of funds, and work stopped. Once they procured more funding, they continued working toward the summit. The inhospitable fall

a high-elevation site was ideal. He knew he must make these observations in late August 1909, when Mars passed sufficiently close to Earth for the first time since 1894.

In 1908, together with astronomer Charles Abbot, Campbell made a brief trip to the summit and determined that a cabin was necessary for scientists to remain for longer observation periods. Funds were obtained from the Smithsonian Institution, and Lone Pine resident Gustave Marsh received the contract to upgrade the Mount Whitney Trail and organize the construction of a research cabin. As with the construction of the trail, Marsh worked efficiently, completing the cabin in less than a month—but still just in time. It was finished on August 27, 1909, and Campbell arrived with his expensive custom instruments the following morning. The measurements he made over the coming days settled the long-running debate, conclusively showing that Mars's atmosphere had, at best, trace amounts of water vapor. Simultaneously, Abbot repeated Langley's solar radiation measurements, obtaining a better estimate of the solar constant. McAdie, the third member of the research party, took meteorological measurements. In 1910 Abbot took additional measurements to refine the solar constant.

The summit cabin was built for those few days of observations in August and September 1909, but it saw sporadic use by astronomers and meteorologists over the following decade. In 1910 Marsh ascended the peak to see Halley's Comet during a lunar eclipse. In 1913 Abbot's Swedish colleague, A. K. Angström, took additional measurements on atmospheric radiation. Since then, the cabin has not been used for research and is now just a reminder of the mountain's vibrant history. In 1977 it was added to the National Register of Historic Places; it is building #77000119 (see nationalregisterofhistoric places.com/CA/Tulare/vacant.html).

weather caused half the workers to abandon the job, and a winter storm in late October forced the others to retreat as well. The next year Gustave Marsh led the construction team. After an additional 10 days of work the following summer, the trail was completed to the summit on July 18, 1904. The crew celebrated with a large bonfire on top—after all, they now had a trail passable by pack stock, which carried the wood to the summit.

In 1909 plans were made to build a research shelter for the Smithsonian Institution atop Mount Whitney, requiring that repairs be made to the trail. Marsh received the contract to construct the summit hut, with the understanding that he would first reestablish the trail where rockslides and avalanches had made the track impassable to stock.

By the early 1920s, however, the trail was again in disrepair due to rockslides, and stock could not reach even the Sierra Crest. Reconstruction began in 1928 as part of an effort to refine the estimated height of Mount Whitney by leveling from Lone Pine to the summit. Crews from Sequoia National Park worked simultaneously on the Mount Whitney Trail and on the newly constructed 67-mile High Sierra Trail. By late 1929, stock parties could once again reach the top of Mount Whitney. In the early 1940s, more work was done on the trail, including the rerouting of the 99 switchbacks to avoid ice fields. Since then, the trail has been maintained, but not much has changed.

What has changed are wilderness ethics. To limit wear on the trail, pack stock was banned in the 1970s, and a camping ban was instituted to protect the fragile lakeshore resources at popular Mirror Lake. Bear canisters are now required, and in 2007, the toilets along the trail were removed, and hikers are now required to pack out their solid waste.

## Natural History

When you take a walk in nature, you are continuously passing stories captured in the plants, animals, rocks, and sky. These stories have two dimensions: first, each organism or rock you pass is named based on its physical characteristics. However, what you see also holds evidence of past events and ongoing processes. The living organisms along the Mount Whitney Trail are there because they have adapted to deal with the long, cold, wet winters and the dry summer months. Unlike those in other alpine regions of the world, most of the plant species here evolved from desert-dwelling species. Some traits, such as the low stature of alpine plants and the small leaves of plants on dry soil, are visible to every passerby, while other traits are physiological in nature and measured by inquisitive scientists. The rocks, likewise, hold clues to their history. For instance, the chemical composition of the rock informs scientists where the rock originated. This section provides an overview of the natural history along the Mount Whitney Trail, and I encourage you to observe as you march along.

## GEOLOGY

The entire Mount Whitney Trail travels over rock known as Whitney granodiorite. Granodiorite is an intrusive igneous rock, meaning that it formed as molten magma solidified belowground. Granodiorite is mostly composed of five minerals: quartz, plagioclase (a type of feldspar), potassium feldspar, hornblende, and biotite. The rock's salt-and-pepper appearance is created by the combination of light-colored quartz and feldspar together with black-colored hornblende and biotite. (Compared to granite, granodiorite has a higher percentage of hornblende and biotite.) Each mineral has a specific chemical composition, shape, and hardness. For instance, the darker-colored minerals have a greater proportion of iron and magnesium than the lighter-colored minerals. In both granodiorite and granite, each mineral's individual crystals are large enough to be seen with the naked eye, indicating that the rock cooled relatively slowly.

To understand how the granodiorite formed, we must turn to plate tectonics. Earth's surface can be divided into at least 15 plates, relatively thin pieces of solid rock (the crust) that float and rotate on the molten material (the mantle) that lies beneath them. As they move, the individual plates may separate, slide past one another, collide, or do any combination of these motions. From about 120 million to 80 million years ago, the Farallon Plate collided with and slid beneath (subducted) the North American Plate. The subducting material was subjected to high temperatures and pressures, causing it and the overlying crust from the North American Plate to melt. Between 88 million and 83 million years ago, some of this material solidified into the rock formations that comprise the Mount Whitney Intrusive Suite, a collection of three irregular-shaped masses of intrusive rock, termed plutons, that includes Whitney granodiorite. These plutons and others comprise the Sierra Nevada batholith (a batholith is a collection of plutons with an exposed surface area greater than 40 square miles).

## HOW WHITNEY GOT ITS HEIGHT

As you climb ever upward, you may wonder how Mount Whitney got so high. Even today, scientific researchers debate this complex issue. What they agree on is that there have been multiple episodes of uplift in the region, each driven by different geologic forces, and each part of the story that created such a tall mountain range.

The pushing of the plutons into place caused the initial uplift of a mountain range, the ancestral Sierra Nevada, in this location. By 80 million years ago, there were imposing volcanic peaks rivaling today's Sierra in height. Amazingly, the approximate locations of the major river drainages were delineated at this time, only then they drained west from Nevada, for the drainage divide was far to the east of today's Sierra Crest. Over the subsequent 50 million years—or even longer—erosion dominated and the ancestral peaks were slowly worn down. It is unknown if steep summits remained or if they were replaced by a more subdued, rolling topography.

A second stage of uplift, which initiated the formation of the mountains we see today, began much more recently, between 10 million and 3 million years ago. Geologists have amassed many lines of evidence indicating an abrupt end to the calm, including increased rates of fault movement and erosion at this time. The main impetus for this uplift appears to have

The crystals comprising the Whitney granodiorite are large compared to the crystals in granites and granodiorites elsewhere in the Sierra. This is because the pluton nests in the middle of the Mount Whitney Intrusive Suite, where the outer layers of rock provided insulation, allowing the magma to cool slowly and the individual crystals to grow larger before the magma solidified completely. Especially noteworthy in the Whitney granodiorite are large crystals of potassium feldspar, termed pegmatites. Rectangular in shape and often measuring 2 inches in each dimension, these crystals protrude from boulders. If you're lucky, you may see a crystal containing concentric rectangles of small dark crystals. These are small hornblende crystals that were engulfed in the more rapidly growing feldspar. Along the Mount Whitney Trail, these large crystals are most common on the slope above the John Muir Trail junction.

been the breaking off of a large piece from the bottom of the crust, a process termed delamination; only in the last two decades has this theory emerged. Having dropped some ballast, the remaining, now thinner, crust became more buoyant and rose. The increased buoyancy enhanced the uplift along faults in the Owens Valley, increasing the height of the Sierra Crest and therefore Mount Whitney. The increased height of the Sierra Crest, relative to California's Central Valley to the west, increased the slope of the western Sierra, increasing erosion rates and deeply incising the existing rivers.

As a result of these events, Mount Whitney eventually "grew" to nearly 11,000 feet above the Owens Valley. But the combined amount of uplift and down-drop on the Sierra Nevada Fault and adjacent Owens Valley Fault are still greater: bedrock in the Owens Valley lies approximately 9,000 feet below the Owens Valley floor, indicating that Mount Whitney actually stands 20,000 feet above the rock under the valley floor. The series of faults in Owens Valley are still active—in 1872 Lone Pine was leveled by an earthquake on the Owens Valley Fault that was estimated to be at least 7.5 on the Richter scale.

What will Whitney's height be in the future? Current evidence suggests that the buoyant response to the delamination is mostly complete in the southern Sierra, while uplift continues more rapidly in the central Sierra.

As you hike up the Mount Whitney Trail, you are likely to see more geologic features than just the evidence of plutons. Here are a few of the highlights:

**Joints:** These natural fractures in the granite formed because the rock contracted as it cooled. The pinnacled profile of the Sierra Crest from Trail Crest to the summit of Mount Whitney is due to jointing. In addition, the regular, large-scale fractures in the rock between the Hitchcock Lakes and Guitar Lake, on the west side of Mount Whitney, are along joints. On a finer scale, the boulders perched on the summit of Mount Whitney formed by jointing. Multiple sets of joints caused the rock to fracture into blocks, which eroded to form fairly rounded giant boulders.

A zoned feldspar crystal embedded in a granite boulder

**Avalanche chutes:** These usually form along joints, where the fractured rock is displaced by water that alternately freezes and thaws in the cracks. The resultant loose rock, often frozen together with snow, is carried downslope by gravity. These avalanches not only remove rock but also polish the chutes. In places, giant slides are truncated some distance above today's valley floor, at the boundary between "steep avalanche chute" and "nearly vertical wall." The bottoms of the much older avalanche chutes were cut off by the more recent glaciers, and this transition marks the height to which the valley was once filled with ice. Avalanche chutes are obvious on the north face of Mount Hitchcock, the steep peak to the southwest of Trail Crest that you see as you walk from Trail Crest to the summit of Mount Whitney.

**Rock glaciers:** Like ice glaciers, rock glaciers—rocks cemented together by ice—move slowly downslope due to gravity. Rock glaciers are often mistaken for moraines (see next entry), as both appear to be poorly sorted collections of boulders. However, rock glaciers are characterized by a notably steep front and often a flattish, rippled top. Along the Mount Whitney Trail, there are several large rock glaciers in the basin east of Mount Whitney, including one just northwest of Trail Camp. Their U-shaped rims are readily visible as you approach the cables on the 99 switchbacks.

**Moraines:** These ridges were formed by the deposition of rocks and other debris carried downslope by a glacier. Lateral moraines form from rocks pushed to the sides of the glacier and are visible along the sides of the valley, while a terminal moraine marks the farthest down-valley extent of the glacier. Along the Mount Whitney Trail, most moraines have been overrun by rock glaciers.

**Glacial polish:** These smooth, shiny surfaces are created when the sediment at the bottom of a glacier scrapes across rock outcrops, evening and smoothing them, and leaving a shiny surface. Meanwhile, coarse rocks dragged along by the glacier may leave grooves and striations. Hunt for sections of glacial polish as you walk along the ridge a little below Trailside Meadow. The boundary between unglaciated and glaciated rock is most obvious if you look north while on the 99 switchbacks: Pinnacle Ridge and the east face of Mount Whitney were not glaciated, while the basin below was.

## VEGETATION

Climbing more than 6,000 feet takes you through four vegetation zones, each of which can be further divided based on the slope's aspect and steepness. Depending on temperature, moisture availability, and other factors, these zones either begin and end abruptly or grade into one another.

**Montane Zone:** Whitney Portal lies in the montane zone, which, in the southern Sierra, extends from about 7,500 feet to just above 9,000 feet. Along the Mount Whitney Trail, low rainfall, the steep aspect, and the resultant coarse, dry soils mean that you will mostly be walking through the montane chaparral community. Drought-resistant evergreen shrubs such as mountain mahogany and bush chinquapin are common members of the community. Meanwhile, small pockets of deep, moister soil host small forest patches inhabited by white fir and Jeffrey pine.

**Subalpine Zone:** The subalpine zone is loosely defined as a region where tree cover thins, although forest cover can still exist—from around 9,500 feet to 11,000 feet in elevation in the Whitney region. The understory is usually sparse and the soil poor. In the southern Sierra, this zone is dominated by lodgepole pine, foxtail pine, and whitebark pine, the latter of which is rare along the Mount Whitney Trail. On flatter slopes, such as near Lone Pine Lake, a dense mono-stand of lodgepole pine is common, while tree cover lessens and picturesque orange-barked foxtail pines become more common in steeper areas. The subalpine zone ends

## JOSIAH DWIGHT WHITNEY

As the supervisor of the California State Geological Survey (the Whitney Survey) between 1860 and 1864, Josiah Dwight Whitney played an important role in the scientific history of the Sierra Nevada. Appointed California state geologist in 1860, he assembled an impressive team of scientists from all disciplines—topography, botany, and geology—to explore and survey the state.

When the surveyors mapped the Sierra during the summers of 1863 and 1864, they were the first nonnatives to visit the southern High Sierra. From the summit of Mount Brewer, they were also the first white men to see the state's highest peak from the west, and they named it after their boss.

The members of the Whitney Survey studied all aspects of California natural history, not just the locations of mineral resources. Unfortunately, California state legislators cared most about finding the location of gold and ended funding for the survey in 1868 when their interests weren't realized. Whitney retained the title of state geologist until 1874, but he returned to the East Coast in 1865 for a professorship at Harvard University.

Today, Whitney is often remembered only for his erroneous belief that Yosemite Valley was not glaciated but created when the valley floor "down-dropped." This led to a lifelong dispute with famous naturalist John Muir, who argued that glaciation was the main mechanism responsible for shaping the Sierra Nevada's landscapes. As the person with greater political power, Whitney forcefully told others that Muir was ignorant and incorrect, stalling the acceptance of Muir's observations, which were later accepted as *mostly* accurate. Whitney was, however, a well-respected, moral scientist— just one who was unwilling to admit a key mistake.

where trees can no longer establish. Along this trail, you will find the last trees about 0.5 mile above Mirror Lake.

**Alpine Zone:** The alpine zone begins above timberline, usually around 11,000 feet in the southern Sierra, and includes only shrubs, herbs, and grasses. In regions with sufficient water, you may encounter meadows, a plant community found along the Mount Whitney Trail only at Trailside Meadow and near Trail Camp. Meadows have a dense cover of grass interspersed with a collection of wildflowers. Elsewhere, ground cover is sparser. In the alpine zone, species composition can be quite varied, depending on small differences in location, as each species has individual requirements for establishment and growth. Many species grow alongside boulders, with their roots seeking the moister soil beneath the rock. Cushion plants are common in sandy flats between rocks, as growing close to the ground alleviates wind chill and the temperatures can be many degrees warmer. As the elevation increases and the growing conditions deteriorate, species diversity declines.

**Barren Rock:** At the highest elevations, no plants can survive. On north-facing slopes, the growing season may be too short, as winter snows may remain on the ground long into summer. On exposed, west-facing slopes, winter temperatures may be too extreme, as winter winds often strip such slopes of all insulating snow cover. Along the last mile to the summit of Mount Whitney, even the sky pilot and alpine gold disappear, as a combination of winter temperatures, winter winds, and growing-season length make the environment too stressful.

Because the Mount Whitney Trail traverses so many vegetation zones, a rich diversity of more than 150 plant species grow alongside the trail. The following is a small subset of those species, selected to represent the ones you are most likely to notice. Some are common along the trail for considerable distances, while others appear only a few places but are abundant and hard to miss. There is a bias toward the higher-elevation species, for it is at these elevations that you will be going the slowest and likely staring at the ground.

The species are listed in the approximate order they appear along the Mount Whitney Trail. For each, I have provided the common name and scientific name (in parentheses), followed by a brief description to aid in identification.

If you are keen to learn the names and natural history stories about more species, pick up a copy of *Wildflowers of the High Sierra and*

*John Muir Trail,* also published by Wilderness Press. Or check out the following website, a wonderful resource with color photos of many of California's plants: calphotos.berkeley.edu/flora.

## HERBS AND SHRUBS

**Curl-leaf mountain-mahogany** (*Cercocarpus ledifolius*): This large shrub dots the slopes adjacent to the trail from Whitney Portal up to approximately 9,200 feet. It becomes less common about halfway between the North Fork of Lone Pine Creek crossing and the Lone Pine Lake junction. It has small, oval-shaped, leathery leaves, but it is most easily distinguished beginning midsummer when it is covered with distinctive seeds: each seed bears a 1-inch, curled tail that is densely covered in branched hairs. These hairs catch the light, giving the entire plant a wonderful glow.

**Fern bush** (*Chamaebatiaria millefolium*): A common large shrub that grows between Whitney Portal and the top of the dry slopes below the Lone Pine Lake junction, this species is named for its much-dissected leaves that resemble fern fronds. The dark-green foliage has a strong odor and is covered with glands and hairs. Its flowers are in elongate clusters at branch ends, the five white petals ringing a dense cluster of yellow stamens (the pollen-producing male reproductive parts).

Poison angelica *(Angelica lineariloba)*

Bridge's penstemon *(Penstemon rostriflorus)*

**Poison angelica** *(Angelica lineariloba)*: A member of the carrot family, poison angelica is common on the slope below the Lone Pine Lake junction. Usually 3–4 feet tall, it bears many small, white flowers in a large, spherical head. As indicated by its scientific name, its leaves are dissected into long, linear lobes.

**Bridge's penstemon** *(Penstemon rostriflorus)*: There are many species of penstemon in the Sierra Nevada, inhabiting environments from wet meadows to high, sandy plateaus. The flowers come in all shades of reds, purples, and blues and are always identifiable by their long, tubular flowers. In the Sierra Nevada, Bridge's penstemon (or scarlet penstemon) is the species with the most vibrant red flowers attached to a single long stalk. Up to 2 feet in height, it is present on many dry, sandy slopes up to 10,500 feet. The Mount Whitney Trail is no exception, and although this species is present until you reach Mirror Lake, it is especially common below the Lone Pine Lake junction.

**Rothrock's keckiella** *(Keckiella rothrockii)*: A relative of the penstemons, this pale-yellow to pinkish, flowered herb is common from Whitney Portal to the top of the switchbacks before the Lone Pine Lake junction. The flowers are smaller than those of Bridge's penstemon and have a broader opening, but they are likewise tubular.

**Inyo meadow lupine** *(Lupinus pratensis)*: This tall lupine occurs in the wet area just downstream of the first crossing of Lone Pine Creek. A member of the pea family, it has mostly purple flowers on elongate flowering stalks. Its 5–10 leaflets are each 1–3 inches long and fuse to a single point—making it palmate, like your hand. The peapodlike fruits are hairy to woolly.

**Mousetail ivesia** (*Ivesia santolinoides*): Along the Mount Whitney Trail, you will see this species only once, but you can't miss the large cluster of these dainty white flowers near the Mount Whitney Zone sign (just beyond the Lone Pine Lake junction). The leaves certainly resemble mouse tails, with 2- to 4-inch stalks of densely clustered, very tiny, hairy leaflets. The flowers occur at the ends of long, spreading stalks, and each of the five petals resembles a miniature rose petal—indeed, this species is a member of the rose family.

**Wavyleaf paintbrush** (*Castilleja applegatei*): A common species on dry slopes throughout the Sierra Nevada from 4,000 feet to 11,000 feet, this paintbrush grows along the Mount Whitney Trail up to around Mirror Lake. It is especially common on the switchbacks just after you enter the Mount Whitney Zone and again on the switchbacks above Outpost Camp. It has heads of red-orange tubular flowers, but if you look closely, you'll see that much of the color is not from the flowers but from the tips of the lobed leaves just below them. This species can always be distinguished from other paintbrushes by its wavy-margined leaves.

**Bush chinquapin** (*Chrysolepis sempervirens*): This shrub, a relative of oaks, grows from Whitney Portal to Mirror Lake. The back side of the leathery leaves is a beautiful golden color, and the fruit is a spiny sphere. It is especially abundant on the switchbacks between Outpost Camp and Mirror Lake.

**Scented shootingstar** (*Primula fragrans*, previously *Dodecatheon redolens*): A common species in wet meadows throughout the subalpine and alpine zones of the southern Sierra Nevada, the scented shootingstar finds few appropriate habitats along the Mount Whitney Trail. You are most likely to notice it in Trailside Meadow, where it is the dominant herb. Its stalks are approximately a foot tall, and its narrow leaves, which attach to the base of the plant, are nearly as long. Its eponymous flowers have five bent-back lavender petals, the trail of the star. The yellow petal bases are fused together, and the stigma and bulky stamens (the female and male reproductive structures) form the tip of the star.

**Cliffbush** (*Jamesia americana*): Appropriately named cliffbush is a light-pink, flowered shrub that often grows in cracks in the cliffs. It has small leaves with serrate tips, and its spreading branches often hug slabs of rock, reminiscent of espaliered fruit trees. Along the Mount Whitney Trail, cliffbush is common between 11,000 feet and 12,000 feet, mostly along the north-facing sides of outcrops.

Sierra primrose *(Primula suffrutescens)*

**Sierra primrose** (*Primula suffrutescens*): This is one of the Sierra's most cheerful flowers, with five bright magenta petals that fuse into a yellow ring. This low-growing shrub emerges at the edge of boulders along the Mount Whitney Trail, mostly between Trailside Meadow and Trail Camp, although a few individuals also grow on the switchbacks above the Mount Whitney Zone sign. The small, slightly fan-shaped leaves have a serrate outer edge.

**Rockfringe** (*Epilobium obcordatum*): Rockfringe joins the Sierra primrose beneath boulders between Trailside Meadow and Trail Camp. It, too, has bright magenta flowers, but they have four large, very thin petals. A late-blooming species with quite small leaves, it emerges from the sandy soil when most other species are already blooming, and its abundant flowers appear only in late summer. (See a photo of it on the next page.)

**Wax currant** (*Ribes cereum*): This shrub, also called squaw currant, is present along the trail from about 11,000 feet to 12,500 feet, disappearing as you approach the section of the switchbacks with the handrail. Like all currants, its leaves resemble maple leaves but with more rounded lobes. By midsummer, the plant bears small, red berries that are edible but not particularly tasty. Unlike most other currants, this species does not have thorns.

**Larger mountain monkeyflower** (*Mimulus tilingii*): Of the approximately 40 species of monkeyflowers in the Sierra Nevada, this is 1 of 3 you will encounter frequently at high elevations. Along the Mount Whitney Trail, it is common between Trailside Meadow

Rockfringe *(Epilobium obcordatum) (see previous page)*

and Trail Camp. Its yellow flowers are tubular, with two petals attached above and three petals arranged below the tube's red-spotted mouth. (The central petal on the bottom is lobed, giving the appearance of two petals.) As with many monkeyflowers, this species grows near trickles of water, both alongside streams and under moist overhangs.

**Sierra cushion wild buckwheat** (*Eriogonum ovalifolium*): This cushion plant becomes common just beyond Trail Camp, growing in sandy patches between boulders. Fine hairs densely cover the leaves, giving the leaf blades a frosted appearance. Spherical heads of small white flowers are borne on 2- to 4-inch stalks. The heads turn pink or reddish by late summer, as the flowers go to seed.

**Cut-leaf fleabane** (*Erigeron compositus*): This small daisy is common throughout the switchbacks. It is best identified by its three-lobed leaves (0.5 inch to an inch in size) because the flowers come in two forms: some are characteristic little daisies, with bright yellow centers surrounded by purple rays, but many lack the rays.

**Gray chickensage** (*Sphaeromeria cana*): Also known as tansy, this relative of the sagebrush grows in sandy patches between boulders along the bottom half of the switchbacks (between 12,000 feet and 13,000 feet), though you may spot a few stragglers west of Trail Crest. It has a disc of minute, cream-colored flowers, which, from a distance, resemble a button.

**Granite draba** (*Draba longisquamosa*): This tiny member of the mustard family is common through the pinnacles along the traverse to the summit and in patches along the 99 switchbacks. The small circles of leaves are especially common near, and even grow in, small trickles of water. The tiny, glossy, almost-fleshy, oval-shaped leaves are rimmed by long, stiff hairs. In June and early July, the plants are covered with small yellow flowers with four petals.

**Dwarf ivesia** (*Ivesia pygmaea*): Like the lower-elevation mousetail ivesia, this species has stalks of closely clustered, miniature leaflets. However, its leaves are not hairy and are therefore a brighter green. Its five-petal, yellow flowers are borne at the end of approximately 2-inch stalks, which emerge from a basal cluster of leaves. Along the Mount Whitney Trail, dwarf ivesia grows mostly at the highest elevations and is most commonly seen toward the top of the switchbacks and near the junction with the John Muir Trail. At these high elevations, it often emerges from cracks in slabs.

**Alpine gold** (*Hulsea algida*): A type of daisy, alpine gold becomes common around 12,500 feet and grows nearly to the summit of Mount Whitney. While most of the species along the switchbacks are small (and bear small flowers), alpine gold has large yellow flowers on 6- to 8-inch stalks. Its rather thick leaves are long, narrow, and gland-dotted, with slightly wavy margins. Despite its strong odor, this species is a favorite food of bighorn sheep and pikas. Along the final miles to the summit, you may encounter small piles of clipped alpine gold leaves. These "hay piles" are left by pikas that are drying the leaves for winter storage.

Alpine gold *(Hulsea algida)*

**Sky pilot** (*Polemonium eximium*): Throughout the Sierra, alpine gold shares the highest habitats with sky pilot. The showiest of High Sierra species, sky pilot boasts a 2- to 3-inch-diameter, spherical head of vibrant purple flowers. The leaves are deeply dissected, have a pungent odor, and are covered with small glands. This species grows among the cliffs on some of the Sierra's highest peaks and is another favorite food of bighorn sheep and pikas.

Sky pilot *(Polemonium eximium)*

## TREES

**White fir** (*Abies concolor*): Growing from Whitney Portal up to around 9,000 feet, the white fir is easily distinguished from pine trees: like all firs, its needles attach singly to the branches. The needles are well over an inch in length, and the bark of the older trees is light in color. Don't expect to find any fir cones lying on the ground, as they disintegrate before they fall.

**Jeffrey pine** (*Pinus jeffreyi*): Jeffrey pines are the towering trees at Whitney Portal that grace the slopes up to about 9,000 feet. Its long needles are bundles in clusters of three, called fascicles, and its large, oval cones are gentle—meaning that the tips of the cone's scales turn inward. Jeffrey pines rarely form a continuous forest cover; instead, they occur singly or in small groups, mostly on dry slopes.

**Lodgepole pine** (*Pinus contorta*): The lodgepole pine is the most common tree in the subalpine Sierra Nevada, forming near monocultures on many flats and on some slopes between 9,000 feet and 11,000 feet. Along the Mount Whitney Trail, the lodgepole pine is most common for the 0.5 mile below the Lone Pine Lake junction, although it occurs occasionally to above Mirror Lake. It is distinguished by needles that are borne in clusters of two; fine, scaly bark; and approximately 1.5-inch, quite spherical cones that are abundant at the base of trees.

**Foxtail pine** (*Pinus balfouriana*): The foxtail pine is a southern Sierra species, common throughout the Kern Basin west of Mount Whitney and more sparingly north. Along the Mount Whitney

Foxtail pine *(Pinus balfouriana)*

Trail, the beautiful orange-barked trees are especially prominent at Outpost Camp, but scattered individuals persist on the slopes above Mirror Lake. These pines are distinguished by long, dangling branches that often have needles only near the tip. The needles, in clusters of five, encircle the stem like a bottlebrush, much like their relatives, the bristlecone pines. The cones are about 3 inches long.

## ANIMALS

Although more than a dozen mammals and at least 50 bird species inhabit the Mount Whitney region, as you traverse the landscape, it appears nearly devoid of wildlife. Most mammals eschew human corridors, and many are nocturnal. Although many bird species are present, they are often seen only at dawn and dusk and even then only identified with the aid of binoculars. Nonetheless, it's difficult to ascend Mount Whitney without seeing a few common alpine (and subalpine) animals and birds. They may include any of the following:

Yellow-bellied marmot

**Yellow-bellied marmots:** The largest mammal commonly seen, the marmot is technically a large, heavyset ground squirrel, approximately 2 feet long (including its bushy tail). In the mid-elevations of the alpine zone, marmots are commonly seen lazing atop boulders, flattening their fat bellies into a thick pancake. They are very common (and aggressive) at Trail Camp.

**Golden-mantled ground squirrels:** About a foot long, approximately a third of which is tail, this brown squirrel, unlike the chipmunk, does not have stripes on its head; the distinct white and black stripes extend only to its neck. Although their stated elevation range is below 10,000 feet, they are common on the Mount Whitney Trail up to Trail Camp.

**Alpine chipmunks:** These tiny, skinny critters are just 6–7 inches long and are easily identified by their small size and face stripes. The highest-elevation chipmunk, they range above 10,000 feet.

**Pikas:** These softball-size balls of fluff have adorable Mickey Mouse ears. Relatives of rabbits, they emit a "peep-peep" when startled; the sound is often the first evidence of their presence, as they quickly scamper into a talus pile. Unlike rodents, pikas do not hibernate during winter. Instead, they subsist beneath the talus on plants they have collected during the summer. If you see a pile of cut plant stems sitting on a rock, it is a pika's hay pile being dried for winter.

**Bighorn sheep:** After numbering only 200 individuals in 1995, Sierra Nevada bighorn sheep are increasing in number, with a healthy population in the Mount Langley area, just south of the Mount Whitney Trail, and a smaller population in the basins to the north. However, the sheep are skittish and rarely stray any closer to the trail than Arc Pass, overlooking Consultation Lake. Nonetheless, a few lucky hikers have seen these most capable mountaineers on the surrounding talus slopes.

**Gray-crowned rosy finches:** Usually observed in small flocks, these finches fly around the alpine landscape in pursuit of insects carried to high elevations by wind currents. When mayfly larvae are hatching into adults, the birds congregate around lakes, gorging themselves. Usually shy, individuals at Trail Camp are remarkably tame as they hop around in search of food.

**Common ravens:** Flying alone or in small groups, the jet-black ravens soar above the summit of Mount Whitney. Take care at Trail Camp, as these stout-beaked birds will approach your food.

**Dark-eyed juncos:** These sparrows, ubiquitous up to and a bit above the treeline, dart in and out of vegetation and are easily distinguished by their blackish heads contrasting against a brownish-grayish body.

Pika

## SOUTHERN SIERRA WEATHER

The southern Sierra Nevada, which includes Mount Whitney, lies between California's Central Valley and Nevada's Great Basin and is primarily influenced by weather from the Pacific Ocean. It experiences a Mediterranean climate with relatively mild, wet winters and warm, dry summers. November–March, Pacific storms bring snow and cold, stormy weather, with temperatures dropping below -20°F in the regions above 10,000 feet. By April, the ferocity of storms declines, and May heralds the return of warm daytime temperatures. However, nights are still chilly, and a large snowpack usually limits access to the backcountry to well-outfitted mountaineers.

In summer, days are often cloudless and temperatures are warm. During July and August, high temperatures are consistently in the 60s at 11,000 feet, with the warmest days creeping toward the mid-70s. The abundant sunshine can make the temperatures feel even warmer. Summer moisture is rare, with rainfall at Crabtree Meadow (a few miles west of Mount Whitney) usually totaling just a few inches between mid-June and mid-September.

The summer moisture that the Sierra does receive comes up from the south, in remnants of tropical storms originating in the Gulf of California, the southeast Pacific Ocean, and even the Gulf of Mexico. Much of the time, this translates into a slow buildup of puffy cumulus clouds, which arrive a bit earlier each afternoon and look a bit more menacing. After a few days, afternoon thunderstorms arrive for a day or two, and then the system disappears again. At times a more intense surge of moisture moves north, bringing a larger pulse of moisture to the eastern Sierra. This can result in a rapid buildup of clouds and/or rain for many hours on end— sometimes even breaking the cardinal rule that "it never rains at night in the Sierra." Any thunderstorm could bring hail to the higher elevations of the Mount Whitney Trail. More important, the lightning that accompanies these storms presents a serious risk to hikers on the exposed upper section of the trail (see more about precautions during lightning storms on page 51).

And of course, when it comes to weather, there is no such thing as normal, only averages. As the astrophysicist Charles Abbot once noted following a very wet, stormy period in August 1909: "One thing was sure, and that was that seasons differ, and while as a rule that location is dry during summer and fall, there are occasional seasons when this is not the case and the 'land of little rain' has to be taken with a grain of salt."

$$\text{\textsc{2}}$$

# Precautions and Considerations

**W**hile a hike up the Mount Whitney Trail is a generally safe endeavor, you should be aware of potential hazards before departing from Whitney Portal. Indeed, all of the items described in this chapter do injure people on this trail each year. Some of the concerns described here are serious medical issues that can result in an emergency situation (for example, hypothermia and altitude sickness), while others are mostly nuisances (for example, blisters). However, because all can keep you from reaching the summit, you'll want to minimize their impact on your trip and learn to recognize the signs that discomfort could be morphing into a dangerous condition.

Perhaps it's because of my background in science, but when I am in the mountains, I like to remind myself of the term *homeostasis*. In reference to our physiology, it is defined as the maintenance of a stable internal environment in the body, despite changes in the external environment. As you hike up Mount Whitney, the external environment is constantly shifting: oxygen availability and temperature decrease with altitude, but your cells need constant amounts

*Above:* Descending toward Trailside Meadow after a successful climb

---

## ACCIDENTS AND INJURIES IN THE SIERRA

If you need one last push to read this section, visit the websites described below. They provide you with real-life stories of injury and death in the Sierra Nevada and generally drive home the reality of dangers in ways that describing the medical conditions cannot. The Inyo County Search & Rescue team website provides details of many accidents and rescues that have occurred on Mount Whitney (and other Sierra peaks) in the past few years (see inyosar.gov, and look under "mission reports"). In addition, the Whitney Zone forum is a great source of information on rescues on the mountain and maintains a featured topic titled "What can go wrong on Whitney" (whitneyzone.com). All told, an average of two people per year have died on Mount Whitney in the past decade, half along the Mount Whitney Trail and the others on various technical routes. Fatalities along the Mount Whitney Trail are attributable to falls, lightning, and preexisting medical conditions.

---

of oxygen and your internal temperature must be maintained at a stable level. In addition, your blood sugar must be maintained, and the concentration of sodium ions, potassium ions, and many other ions must also be maintained at a constant level. Although the body does a very good job fine-tuning internal conditions, you have to supply it with the essential materials: oxygen, food, and water.

It is also important that you have the knowledge, experience, and gear to appropriately respond to changes in your external environment. This section covers the fundamentals you need to consider to avoid physiological problems such as altitude sickness, hypothermia, dehydration, electrolyte depletion, and other potential hazards such as lightning, injuries, and blisters.

## Altitude Sickness

"If you feel unwell at altitude, it is altitude illness until proven otherwise." This first golden rule of altitude sickness reminds you that this condition is the hazard most likely to affect you on your hike up Mount Whitney. According to one study conducted during July and August 2006, more than half of the people attempting to summit Mount Whitney via the Mount Whitney Trail suffered from the form of altitude sickness known as acute mountain sickness (AMS), a collection of symptoms, including a headache, that occurs when a person rapidly ascends to high altitude.

Many people on the Mount Whitney Trail plan a rapid ascent (and descent), thinking they don't need to worry about the more severe forms of altitude sickness: high-altitude cerebral edema (HACE), or swelling in your brain caused by a buildup of fluid, and high-altitude pulmonary edema (HAPE), or swelling in your lungs caused by a buildup of fluid, because these usually take more than 12 hours to develop. Just keep the *usually* in mind; there are cases of HACE and HAPE along the Mount Whitney Trail, and they often require emergency evacuations. Even relatively mild AMS can impair your judgment, and there is no way to quantify how many accidents are caused by poor decisions people made because of AMS. After personally evacuating a solo hiker likely suffering from HACE from the summit of Mount Whitney, I will never forget the gravity of the symptoms. See the sidebar "A Slow Descent of Mount Whitney," on page 34, for the story.

What follows is a description of how the body responds to decreased oxygen availability and a summary of the symptoms of AMS, HACE, and HAPE. This information is an overview only; if you wish to learn more, I strongly recommend Charles Houston's *Going Higher* (Mountaineers Books, 2005), *Altitude Illness: Prevention & Treatment* by Stephen Bezruchka (Mountaineers Books, 2005), the Altitude Research Center website (altituderesearch.org), and the Facebook group Altitude Acclimatization, which maintains a good collection of resources with a focus on the Sierra Nevada.

## CAUSES OF ALTITUDE SICKNESS

The root cause of altitude sickness is hypoxia, the insufficient supply of oxygen to the body's tissues. Earth's atmosphere becomes thinner at higher elevations because, with increasing altitude, there is less weight, and therefore less pressure, exerted by the atmosphere above. As a result, the air at high elevation is less dense than the air at sea level, and thus gases in the atmosphere, including oxygen, are more spread out. At the summit of Mount Whitney, there is 58% as much oxygen in a given volume as there is at sea level.

Hemoglobin is the protein in red blood cells that carries oxygen to all of the body's cells. As the partial pressure of oxygen in the air

*Continued on page 38*

## A SLOW DESCENT OF MOUNT WHITNEY

I hope that reading the following true story helps others avoid finding themselves in this situation. Several poor decisions combined to create this emergency situation: hiking solo—in particular, hiking solo when you have a history of altitude problems—and continuing to the summit late in the day.

In August 2013 my husband, Douglas, and I spent a week hiking southbound along the John Muir Trail (JMT) corridor. We decided to spend our last night at the small bivvy sites near the junction with the JMT and the Mount Whitney Trail, 2 miles before the summit. Dropping our big packs, we then headed to the summit to enjoy the evening light, arriving around 6 p.m. A little below the summit I noted a lone hiker sitting, head bent downward, and made a half-conscious mental note to make sure he'd moved onward by the time we descended. We spent a lovely hour on the summit, chatting with other hikers we'd crossed paths with along the JMT, and then headed down to reach our camp by dark.

We'd walked only 5 minutes when we came upon the same hiker, sitting in the same slouched position, only about 200 feet down the trail from where he was an hour earlier. I noted to Douglas that we needed to check how he was doing. His response to my queries on his well-being was an unconvincing "fine," and we probed further. He knew his name, he wasn't sure if he had any water or food left to consume, he wasn't sure how long he'd been sitting there or when he'd left Whitney Portal, and he was tired and wanted to rest. We looked at each other and knew the answer was "get down now." At this point one of us should maybe have headed back up to the summit to borrow someone's cell phone and alert authorities to his condition, but at the time we discounted the idea because it was already too late to initiate a helicopter evacuation. We also assumed that he would be able to walk downward if we motivated him and worked on getting food and water in him, and we didn't want to waste any daylight. My thought at this time was that one of us would walk with him to Trail Crest and by then he'd be able to keep moving on his own. For the first mile, we made slow but steady progress—it took an hour. He drank a little, he ate a little, and he would walk for a minute or two before sitting for a few seconds. He did have sufficient clothes—several layers on top, gloves, and a warm hat. He was not overweight and seemed fit. One of the first things I noticed was his lack of balance, ataxia, but also that he had clearly hiked a fair bit because he picked his foot placement well on the rocky trail. However, if he had to step over a rock or down a little more than usual, his balance was atrocious and we'd have to help him. The sun set as we passed around the base of Keeler Needle. The traverse across the pinnacles went on and on, and I needed Douglas to help balance him whenever there was a drop-off because I didn't trust that, if he fell, he wouldn't push me off the trail. The fact that he was suffering from the early symptoms of high-altitude cerebral edema (HACE) became ever clearer in my mind.

By this point I was watching the final hints of deep red and blue above the Kaweah Peaks and knew it would soon be very dark. Luckily we all had headlamps. Douglas and I now realized that someone needed to help him get down to Trail Camp for the night—and that someone was us. It was a chilly, windy evening, and we didn't have the spare gear to outfit him at 13,500 feet. And we were fairly certain that he needed to get even lower. Once past the pinnacles, Douglas ran back to camp to cook some hot soup for all of us and pack his pack. He met us at the trail junction with steaming cups. This has to have been a savior, for with the hot, salty drink and noodles in his stomach, our friend made it up the 200-foot climb to Trail Crest with relatively little trouble. He and Douglas had just reached the pass when I caught up to them—having detoured briefly to get my own pack. It was now between 9 and 9:30 p.m., and Douglas and I breathed a premature sigh of relief. We'd done the 2-mile flat traverse and the brief uphill. Now it was just downhill and we'd be at even lower elevations. Our friend had a cell phone (we didn't), and from Trail Crest we tried to call his wife—who was purportedly waiting for him at Whitney Portal—simply to indicate our location and that he was with others. The connection went through but then cut out before we could speak to her. We also tried to call the sheriff with a similar outcome.

Our spirits may initially have been high, but those 2 miles had obviously sapped the last energy our friend could muster, and his pace rapidly lessened. I think the pitch-blackness around

*(Continued on page 36)*

(Continued from page 35)

him was also disorienting, exacerbating his mental difficulties. Douglas and I have been up and down the trail enough times—and simply have a good sense of our surroundings—so we knew exactly where we were: going down a good trail on the east side of Mount Whitney. Our goal, Trail Camp, was a mere 2.2 miles below us, about an hour on a good day. Our friend, however, became very concerned that we were leading him astray. He could no longer see Mount Whitney—or anything beyond the beam of his headlamp, and began asking us why we were still making him walk when we'd climbed down the mountain. He said he understood why we'd made him walk down the mountain to the nearest campsite, and he appreciated that, but now we'd gotten there, so why did we have to keep going? Why were we torturing him by making him walk around and around in circles? Were we kidnapping him and were then going to murder him? Our answers weren't very creative—I guess we were past thinking outside the box—and we simply tried to reassure him that we were helping him and would be there "soon."

The pace of the walk was surreal. I had my GPS running, to have some sense of progress, but it was painful being excited about each 10-foot descent in altitude. It also made me realize just how sick this man was. Even my kids as preschoolers at their most tired could always summon more energy than this to reach a destination. We'd sit for long periods and finally urge him to stand up, hold his hand, and lead him onward, only to have him collapse on a rock again after 20 steps. The colder it became, the harder it was. We were wearing all our layers but still cold. While I never once regretted our decision to walk him down, mixed into all this were our emotions of being a little miffed at having given up our lovely alpine perch on our final night of our trip and now a night of sleep. The less cooperative he became, the harder it was for me to keep urging him on. Being told again and again that I was torturing him and kidnapping him was difficult to stomach. Eventually Douglas and I began taking turns for 10 minutes, while one of us could sit on our own. We made sure never to get mad at him, only to try and explain that he was sick and we were helping him. We explained that we were both experienced in the mountains and were good people to be with him. We told him that as soon as we reached the campsite, he'd get to sleep as much as he wanted. But hearing the same concerns about being kidnapped and murdered voiced again and again wore us down. The hours just kept ticking by, and we moved slower and slower. He begged us to just let him rest and sleep, and we contemplated it but knew that it was an unusually cold night and the slopes were steep. What if we fell asleep and he got up, stumbled, and fell? Once below the icy section with the handrail, the terrain is a bit more moderate, and we started looking for little nooks but never settled on one, for it didn't seem like a sensible plan—and we weren't able to detach ourselves enough from wanting all of us to reach Trail Camp to formulate an alternative plan. So on we walked.

Around 1 a.m. we were about 500 feet above Trail Camp and were questioning how much longer we could continue without voicing any frustration with the situation—for us it was about being cold and not making much progress, not exhaustion, fortunately. We could see some lights still on in tents and decided that we needed a relief team. We decided that we were close enough to the bottom now that if we summoned others to help us for a few hours, we wouldn't jeopardize their summit attempts in the morning. Douglas walked ahead and called in at the first tent he reached, explaining the situation and requesting help. Two guys rapidly emerged and good-humoredly agreed to relieve me. They did what I was unable to—break the spell, by having an everyday conversation with our friend. What were his favorite movies? What were his hobbies? Suddenly he felt comfortable, the images of being murdered faded, and he picked up the pace a little and worked his way down to Trail Camp, arriving between 2 and 2:30 a.m. In the meantime I got to go ahead. Douglas and I found a free place to pitch our tent—we'd already agreed that our friend would get the tent, my Therm-a-Rest, and an emergency blanket, while we'd sleep outside. Upon reaching Trail Camp, he readily climbed into our tent and was soon asleep. We crossed our fingers that he'd be OK in the morning.

Douglas slept on his Therm-a-Rest and me on our two backpacks. I slept fitfully—at best—even after the first hikers rose

*(Continued on page 38)*

*(Continued from page 37)*

at 4 a.m. and handed me a Therm-a-Rest on which to sleep. My sleeping bag was completely inadequate to break the wind and I shivered and shivered. At first light I got up and began to pace around. I'd have loved to have passed the time by hiking up Wotans Throne, but I knew we had to stay put to greet our friend when he emerged. Around 6:30 a.m. he got up. Amazingly, he was happy, coherent, and understood completely what had happened the night before. He apologized for saying things he didn't mean. And he stared and stared up at the switchbacks and said, "You walked down all of those with me in the night?" We nodded and he thanked us again and again, very aware that he'd been in a bad state and couldn't have gotten down on his own. As we talked over breakfast, we were amazed at the change in him and all the things he could tell us in 15 minutes that he couldn't during 7 hours the night before. We had an interesting, intelligent conversation, which really drove home my appreciation for how impaired his mental capacity had been the night before. After breakfast he headed down the trail and we followed soon thereafter. When we passed him near Trailside Meadow, he was all smiles.

*Continued from page 33*

you breathe decreases, the amount of oxygen available for the tissues in your body decreases, leading to hypoxia.

The body has a complex response to the low barometric pressure, and resultant low oxygen pressure, with just about every organ affected and in a multitude of ways. In the brain, stress hormones—and other factors—cause increased blood flow, leading to increased blood supply (and blood pressure) to the capillaries, the smallest blood vessels, in the brain. The capillaries begin to leak, which leads to swelling (edema) of the brain and causes brain tissue to get crushed against the cranium. AMS occurs when this swelling is minor, while HACE is diagnosed when this swelling is particularly severe. In the lungs, constriction of the pulmonary vessels increases resistance to blood flow. In some cases, this leads

Once I reached Whitney Portal and spoke with other hikers and the man's wife, I learned more. He knew he had altitude problems. A year earlier he had attempted the peak as an overnight trip with his wife and had turned back at Trail Camp because of altitude problems. For this Whitney attempt he had begun at 10 p.m. for a day hike the following day—on his own. He had spent the previous days hiking at elevation to acclimate and had felt good when he started. Other hikers around Whitney Portal could say that by morning, he'd been on the switchbacks above Trail Camp, and by 2 p.m. hikers had seen him "barely moving" approaching the summit. He was still heading up at that point because he signed the summit register only a few people ahead of us. I don't know if others had asked if he needed help, but his "I'm fine" would have been much easier to accept in the middle of the day, with dozens of others nearby, than at 7 p.m., when we knew we were the last people descending that day. Several hours earlier, we'd probably have ignored it as well.

By the way, I've corresponded with this man a few times since. He's fine and continuing to hike, just sticking to somewhat lower elevations.

A longer version of this can be found in the archives of the Altitude Acclimatization Facebook page.

to increased fluid leakage from the capillaries into the tissues and air spaces (alveoli) in the lungs—or HAPE. The fluid reduces the area across which gas is exchanged, exacerbating hypoxia. Also contributing to the body's responses to hypoxia are hormones secreted from the kidneys that cause sodium (salt) retention, which in turn causes fluid retention and swollen hands and feet.

Altitude sickness is fickle, affecting the same person differently on different occasions. It is known that certain people are more likely to suffer from altitude sickness than others, but physicians still don't know what makes a person prone to altitude sickness. Indeed, if you do not intimately know your own body's response to increased elevation, you both need to be extravigilant of AMS symptoms and make even more of an effort to acclimate your body before ascending Mount Whitney. Note also that even very fit people get altitude sickness.

## SYMPTOMS OF ALTITUDE SICKNESS

AMS is actually a collection of symptoms on a continuum that, at its more severe end, includes HACE. If you are at high elevation, you by definition have AMS if you have a moderate headache together with one or more of the following symptoms:

- loss of appetite, nausea, or vomiting
- fatigue or weakness
- dizziness or light-headedness
- difficulty sleeping

See the sidebar "Lake Louise Scoring" on page 42 for a standardized way to self-evaluate your symptoms.

Other symptoms that may occur when you have AMS include shortness of breath, low urine output, and peripheral edema (swelling of the feet, legs, and/or hands).

HACE, a severe form of AMS, is characterized by more acute edema in the brain. In addition to more extreme AMS symptoms, individuals with HACE have mental confusion and a loss of coordination. If a member of your party appears to be developing these symptoms (for example, cannot walk in a straight line—the classic

---

## HOW THE BODY ACCLIMATES TO HYPOXIA

The body uses many interlinked processes to compensate for hypoxia, some immediate and some longer term. These allow most individuals to successfully acclimate to elevations of about 17,000 feet over the course of a month. On a long weekend climb of Mount Whitney, your body will just be starting to adjust, which is why it is important to begin acclimating in advance. Three processes important to acclimation are:

**Hyperventilation:** At higher elevations, there are fewer oxygen molecules in each breath. This leads to an increased rate of breathing, known as the hypoxic ventilatory response. This continues for many weeks at altitude and is very important for maintaining higher blood oxygen levels.

**Increased blood alkalinity and increased output of bicarbonate in urine:** Breathing faster causes the blood to off-load more carbon dioxide to the capillaries in the lungs, increasing blood alkalinity (higher pH). However, higher blood pH leads to a negative feedback response: a decreased rate "drunken sailor" walk), he or she must descend immediately. HACE can lead to death within days or even hours. Although AMS symptoms usually precede HACE, HACE symptoms can develop quite suddenly in a person who previously had no symptoms ascribable to altitude sickness.

HAPE symptoms include a cough, decreased performance, chest congestion, and shortness of breath while at rest. The often mentioned symptoms of severe respiratory distress—coughing up blood and gurgling sounds in the chest—occur later in the progression of the condition. Note that HAPE diagnosis does not require a headache. As with HACE, an individual with these symptoms must descend rapidly. The majority of altitude sickness fatalities are due to HAPE. It is more common in men than in women and can appear in people well acclimated to high elevations if they descend to low elevations for just a few days before reascending.

## PREVENTING ALTITUDE SICKNESS

There are many actions you can take to reduce your risk of AMS:

- **Stay well hydrated—but not overhydrated.**

---

of breathing countering the hypoxic ventilatory response. Because the body needs to maintain the high breathing rate to take in more oxygen, it must counter the higher blood pH. It does this by excreting bicarbonate, an alkaline compound, via the kidneys, shifting blood alkalinity back toward normal. This relatively slow response continues for several days and is probably the main form of acclimation on a trip that lasts a few days to a week.

The prescription drug acetazolamide (Diamox) speeds up this process (and allows it to begin at low elevations) by increasing bicarbonate excretion and by increasing blood carbon dioxide levels, thus causing increased ventilation and increased intake of oxygen. It is also a diuretic and enhances sodium excretion, helping to decrease peripheral swelling.

**Increased red blood cell count:** Although this response begins immediately, it takes your body many weeks to increase its red blood cell count enough to offset the decrease in oxygen availability.

## LAKE LOUISE SCORING

The Lake Louise Score is a way for people to self-report acute mountain sickness symptoms and assess the severity of their condition. It is used worldwide by people ascending to high elevations.

Add together the individual scores for each symptom to get the total score. A total score of:

3–5 = mild AMS
6 or more = severe AMS

**HEADACHE**
- No headache = 0
- Mild headache = 1
- Moderate headache = 2
- Severe headache, incapacitating = 3

**GASTROINTESTINAL SYMPTOMS**
- None = 0
- Poor appetite or nausea = 1
- Moderate nausea and/or vomiting = 2
- Severe nausea and/or vomiting = 3

**FATIGUE AND/OR WEAKNESS**
- Not tired or weak = 0
- Mild fatigue/weakness = 1
- Moderate fatigue/weakness = 2
- Severe fatigue/weakness = 3

**DIZZINESS/LIGHT-HEADEDNESS**
- Not dizzy = 0
- Mild dizziness = 1
- Moderate dizziness = 2
- Severe dizziness, incapacitating = 3

**DIFFICULTY SLEEPING**
- Slept as well as usual = 0
- Did not sleep as well as usual = 1
- Woke many times, poor sleep = 2
- Could not sleep at all = 3

- **Eat enough food.**

- **Know your body.** There are two parts to this. First, people who have had previous episodes of altitude sickness have a much higher risk of suffering from it. Second, know what you feel like when you are simply hiking hard and exhausted, so you can accurately attribute "different" symptoms to AMS.

- **Ascend slowly.** Although it is rarely followed by hikers on the Mount Whitney Trail, the often-stated rule for reducing risk of AMS is that, above 10,000 feet, you should ascend no more than 1,000 feet per night. This suggests that overnight hikers should spend one night at Outpost Camp and a second night at Trail Camp before continuing to the summit. Most people will choose not to adopt this plan for Mount Whitney because it takes an extra day to reach the summit. However, if you have a history of AMS, an ascent spread over more days might help.

- **Get a good night's sleep before your hike.** Don't drive up after work, arrive in Lone Pine at 1 a.m., and begin hiking a few hours later.

- **Take the time to acclimate.** This is quite simply the most important altitude sickness prevention—it is inadvisable to plan to ascend to 14,505 feet without both knowing how your body responds to high elevation and giving yourself several days to acclimate. Beginning on page 65, there are suggestions of nearby day hikes that take you to elevations of 10,000 and 12,000 feet. Going high during the day and then sleeping at lower elevations helps your body acclimate faster and generally makes you feel better, because at night you'll be able to sleep and eat well. Sleeping low does not mean that you have to retreat to Lone Pine for the night. If you plan on camping, a good plan would be to sleep at Whitney Portal (elevation 8,330 feet) the night before your hike. Most people sleep well at Whitney Portal, while the moderate elevation allows the body to continue acclimating for their excursion up the Mount Whitney Trail. Alternatively, you could stay at one of the 10,000-foot campgrounds at Horseshoe Meadows (see page 101).

- **If you do experience altitude sickness on your hike, follow the second golden rule:** never ascend with symptoms of AMS. Because more than a third of people climbing Mount Whitney experience symptoms before reaching the summit, many people clearly ignore this advice each year. Yet very few develop symptoms indicative of HAPE or HACE, probably due to the short period of time hikers are at the highest elevations. If you choose to continue upward despite AMS symptoms, be aware of the risks, monitor yourself (and have your hiking partners monitor you), and descend immediately if your symptoms worsen.

- **If you plan to take a prescription drug,** such as acetazolamide, make sure you know your body's reaction to it ahead of time.

- **Descent is the best cure.** Almost all altitude sickness symptoms disappear immediately when you retreat to lower elevations.

## MEDICAL TREATMENTS FOR ALTITUDE SICKNESS

Although it's by no means necessary if you prepare and acclimate properly, many people climbing Mount Whitney elect to take medication—mostly aspirin/ibuprofen, and occasionally prescription drugs—in hopes of decreasing their susceptibility to or symptoms of altitude sickness. Some of these medications are described below. Note: If you choose to pursue any drugs, prescription or otherwise, please do so under the care of a medical doctor, and be sure to research the contraindications and side effects of any medication you plan to take.

**Aspirin and ibuprofen:** Both of these anti-inflammatory drugs help relieve headaches, although many people prefer ibuprofen because it is effective in smaller doses. Taking an anti-inflammatory drug preventively may keep you from feeling lousy due to a headache. If you feel better, you also tend to eat and drink more, which may further minimize altitude sickness.

**Acetazolamide:** This prescription medication (the main brand name is Diamox) helps your body acclimate by acidifying your blood, which stimulates breathing. People who use this drug usually begin taking it a day or two before ascending to high elevations to give the body a head start on the acclimation process. Common side effects include more frequent urination and a tingling sensation in the toes and fingers. People who are sensitive to sunlight or sulfa drugs may have additional side effects and should consult a doctor about their allergies and sensitivities. It is recommended that you take acetazolamide at home, before your trip, to ensure you do not have any severe side effects. Note, as well, that when taken as a preventive measure, acetazolamide is generally taken in smaller doses than when taken to relieve existing symptoms.

**Dexamethasone:** This prescription drug is a corticosteroid thought to increase oxygenation and therefore reduce symptoms of edema in blood vessels. It may therefore decrease brain swelling and is used to treat severe symptoms of AMS and HACE. Dexamethasone is only effective as a treatment for HAPE if taken prior to ascent. Dexamethasone is usually carried on high-altitude expeditions but rarely prescribed preventively at Sierran elevations. Side effects can include an upset stomach, high blood sugar, and mood changes.

# Hypothermia

Hypothermia is a potentially lethal condition that results from an abnormally low body temperature. Usually presumed to occur at cold temperatures, it can happen at an air temperature as high as 70°F, especially if the person is wet from rain or sweat or the conditions are windy. Because temperatures on the Mount Whitney Trail between Trail Camp and the summit rarely rise above 70°F, hypothermia is a possibility to take seriously when planning your hike. Hypothermia can occur with little warning and rapidly leads to a loss of mental function, which is why you must be aware of the early symptoms. You should constantly monitor yourself and group members for symptoms if attempting the summit on a cold, wet, or windy day. It is because of these very real dangers that you should carry extra clothes and a space blanket up the mountain.

Hypothermia sets in when the core body temperature drops below 95°F, only a 3.6°F decrease from normal. The first symptom is shivering—the body's attempt to rewarm itself. Signs of confusion and difficulty speaking may occur when the core temperature drops below 94°F. In the advanced stages of hypothermia, shivering stops, the body's core temperature drops below 90°F, and a person may no longer feel cold. He or she will become incoherent, with severely limited judgment. Death can result if body temperature drops below 80°F.

Mild hypothermia can be treated in the field, while severe hypothermia must be treated in a medical facility so the patient can be rewarmed properly. Poor heart function and sudden cardiac death are possible if a severely hypothermic patient is not handled carefully. This makes it imperative to catch and reverse mild hypothermia before the condition worsens.

If an injury (or poor planning) forces you to spend a night on the mountain, if your clothes get wet in a storm, or if you are underdressed on a cold, windy day, you are at severe risk of hypothermia. Here are a few ways to minimize your chances of becoming hypothermic:

- Wear a hat. A large proportion of heat is lost through the head.
- If you end up with wet clothes, change into dry clothes immediately.
- If you are waiting for group members and find yourself getting cold, put on extra clothes, move out of the wind, and pace back and forth, swinging arms and legs vigorously to enhance circulation.
- If you are forced to spend a night on the mountain, find a sheltered location out of the wind, and huddle together with other group members, minimizing the surface area exposed to the cold conditions.

If you suspect someone in your group is hypothermic:

- Get the individual into a location sheltered from the wind.
- Make sure the person is wearing warm, dry clothes.
- If the patient is conscious and can swallow, feed the person warm, sweet liquids or easily digested foods.
- If possible, the hypothermic person should be put in a prewarmed sleeping bag, with warm water bottles placed inside.
- Monitor the patient's pulse, breathing, and, if possible, body temperature. Plan for an evacuation if the patient does not improve. If the condition is severe, get help

immediately. Also remember that severely hypothermic patients may appear to lack a pulse, but that does not mean the person is deceased.

## Hydration

Dehydration is yet another ailment that leads to headaches and low energy. The body needs to maintain a constant amount of water in its cells and tissues to function, as well as to effectively transport blood and oxygen to the organs. While hiking, you will lose water by urinating, by sweating, and through respiration. The latter can be greatly exacerbated at high altitude because you breathe more rapidly and the air is very dry.

HINT: I prefer the flavor of plain water while hiking, so instead of filling a whole bottle with an energy drink, I bring a small cup and bag of electrolyte mix and mix a cup during a few of my longer breaks.

However, it is also unhealthy to drink too much water, which can upset the balance of electrolytes in your body. You must keep up with water loss, but do not overdo it. Even under much hotter desert conditions, 8 quarts per day is generally adequate, and 5–9 quarts during a one-day ascent of Mount Whitney (or nearly twice as much during a two-day ascent) should suffice for most people. Consume your water slowly and continually throughout the day. Many people report not feeling thirsty, especially in cool weather, so force yourself to drink at least 1–2 cups of water an hour. A good indicator of being hydrated is simply the need to urinate every few hours.

If your water intake does not keep pace with water loss, the initial signs of dehydration include thirst, dry mouth, fatigue, dark urine, dry skin, and loss of appetite. As the condition worsens, you may note nausea, headaches, muscle cramps, increased respiration and heart rate, and decreased sweating and urination. If a member of your group gets dehydrated, have that person take a break and slowly drink water with electrolytes. Severe dehydration requires medical attention.

## Food

You will burn approximately 6,000 calories during your one-day ascent of Mount Whitney and about 9,000 calories during a two-day journey. Although you're unlikely to consume that many calories on your walk, don't skimp on food to save weight.

Food provides the body with the molecules the cells—including the cells in the muscles—use as energy. Food is also the body's source of various ions, or electrolytes. It's important to eat frequently as you exert yourself, because your muscle cells will run out of glycogen (stored carbohydrates). Indeed, a carbohydrate-heavy diet is recommended for mountain walking.

*Electrolytes* is a catchall term for a collection of salts, including sodium, potassium, and calcium; the relative concentrations of these

## WATERBORNE PESTS

Unless you plan to carry all the water you need for your hike (approximately 5–9 quarts), you'll need to obtain water on the trail. The southern fork of Lone Pine Creek sees such heavy use that most hikers choose to treat water along the Mount Whitney Trail to prevent contamination with protozoa, such as giardia or cryptosporidium, or bacteria such as *E. coli.* Viruses do not survive long in the cold, harsh conditions of the alpine environment and are unlikely to infect water in the Sierra Nevada. (As described on page 83, most hikers will choose to carry only 2 quarts at a time and purify along the way to reduce the weight they are carrying.)

If you choose not to treat your water, there are several sources that, until they intersect the Mount Whitney Trail, do not pass through heavily used areas. They include a spring in Bighorn Park, east of Outpost Camp; the outlet from Mirror Lake; and the spring that appears about 400 feet above Trail Camp. (If you're curious to read more about Sierra water quality, see articles by Dr. Robert Derlet and Dr. Robert Rockwell in the Yosemite Association's "Nature Notes" archive [sierranature notes.com] or at whitneyzone.com/docs/BobR/Giardia.pdf. These articles show that, in most of the Sierra, water quality is incredibly good, and with careful water selection, treating water before drinking is not essential.)

As you pick a water treatment method, keep in mind that different treatments kill or remove different microbes:

- **Chemical purification (for example, iodine or chlorine):** This is the easiest method of treating water—simply add drops or a tablet—but you have to wait about 20 electrolytes is essential in maintaining nerve and muscle function, blood acidity, hydration, and the delivery of oxygen to your cells.

While your kidneys do a good job of balancing the relative concentrations of the different electrolytes, they can do their job only if the electrolytes are present in your body. It's up to you to consume sufficient food. As you hike, stop frequently and eat small amounts of food every 1–2 hours. Carry a variety of appetizing snacks to entice yourself to eat when tired, cold, or suffering from altitude mountain

---

minutes to drink your water. Some chemical purification methods leave a distinct chemical flavor, while others do not. In addition, chemical purification might not kill cryptosporidium, so if this microbe becomes more common in the Sierra, this method will no longer be practical.

- **Water filter:** Water filters should remove all bacteria and protozoa, but the pores of many filters are too large to remove viruses. The advantages of filtering are that it removes all microorganisms of concern (in the Sierra Nevada) and doesn't leave a flavor in your water. But it can be time-consuming. If you are part of a large group with a single water filter, make sure the filter is in continuous use during your break, because you can lose a lot of time if many people need to filter right when you want to start walking.

- **Squeeze filter:** Squeeze filters (for example, Sawyer Mini) are filters that screw straight onto your water bottle. You effectively purify the water as you drink. They are lightweight and allow each person to easily carry his or her own filter, but some brands clog easily and have quite low flow.

- **Ultraviolet-light purifier (for example, SteriPEN):** Ultraviolet light damages the DNA of all microorganisms, rendering them harmless. Water must be clear for the ultraviolet light to function, so water with silt must be filtered. And make sure you have spare batteries with you.

- **Boiling:** Boiling kills all microorganisms but is very time-consuming, requires a stove and fuel, and is not practical for day hikers.

## POOR METABOLIC FUNCTION

Metabolism is the sum of all the chemical and physical processes that occur in the body to turn food you eat and the
oxygen you breathe into energy that the body can use. These
processes occur within the cells, and metabolic function can
decrease if there is an insufficient supply of food and oxygen
to the cells, or if the cells are not effectively using the food
and oxygen they receive.

The link between high elevation and hypoxia, a deficiency
in the amount of oxygen reaching the body's tissues, to
metabolic function is obvious. However, other conditions—
including dehydration, hypothermia, and electrolyte
depletion—also, by complex physiological pathways, cause
poor metabolic function by affecting the supply of substances
to the cells and the use of substances by the cells.

Because all of these conditions make cells less efficient at
metabolizing food and oxygen, they physiologically reinforce
one another, exacerbating the poor cellular function caused
by other conditions. This means that if you are dehydrated or
low on electrolytes, you are more likely to display symptoms
associated with poor metabolic function. For instance, headaches at high elevation are generally attributed to altitude
sickness. However, they may be due, in part, to dehydration
and not eating enough.

sickness (AMS). Consider what you might find appealing if you're
nauseated—that tuna fish sandwich might not sound as appealing at 14,000 feet as it did at sea level. Stop and eat a large snack
no higher than Trail Camp—if you are suffering from AMS, your
desire (or ability) to eat will decrease as you continue your ascent
and it is best to have refueled your body in advance. While exercis-
ing, your body constantly loses electrolytes by sweating, especially
on a hot day. Salty food and electrolyte-containing energy drinks
will help your body replenish its lost electrolytes. Just check the
ingredients in the energy drink you choose to make sure it contains
sodium, the electrolyte whose loss is most likely to cause medical
problems. Finally, beware of drinking too much plain water, which
can throw off your electrolyte balance, especially if you're not eating adequately.

# Lightning

From the switchbacks west of Trail Camp all the way to the summit of Mount Whitney, the trail is exposed, leaving hikers vulnerable to lightning strikes. Moreover, should a storm suddenly develop, there is no escape route along the last 2 miles to the summit. Byrd Surby, the first recorded fatality on Mount Whitney, was killed by lightning near the summit in 1904, just eight days after the Mount Whitney Trail was completed. Lightning on or near the summit has actually killed very few people, but more have been struck and sustained injuries of varying severity.

As described in the weather section on page 30, thunderstorms are much rarer in the Sierra Nevada than in most other mountain ranges, and it is often safe to be at high elevations throughout the day. However, if tall cumulus clouds develop when you are on the mountain, it is imperative that you watch them closely and descend if they approach.

Before you begin your hike, check the weather forecast at the National Oceanic and Atmospheric Administration website: go to www.wrh.noaa.gov/vef, and click on a location due south of Bishop and a bit north of the latitude of Death Valley. If the probability of precipitation is 10%, it is my experience that you will stay dry 75% of the time, but you need to get a very early start to safely summit Mount Whitney. If the probability of precipitation is listed as 20%, you will get wet more than half the time and should accept from the outset that you may not be able to summit. Only if the probability of precipitation is 30% (or greater) is rain very likely.

Regardless of the forecast, turn around promptly when you see tall, dark, flat-bottomed cumulonimbus (thunder) clouds nearby. Clouds can build very quickly: scattered white clouds can evolve into a nasty storm in less than 2 hours, less time than it takes most people to hike round-trip from Trail Crest to the summit. It takes even less time for a seemingly distant storm to move overhead. If you hear even distant thunder, head down quickly. In clear air, thunder can be heard from a distance of approximately 10 miles. (While lightning can move vertically through the sky and can strike while there is clear sky above, this is rare and is not a major concern.)

Lightning occurs to alleviate charge imbalances between the clouds (usually negative) and the ground (usually positive). These imbalances develop because negative and positive charges are separated within clouds, leading to charged water molecules. The negative charges within a thundercloud cause equal positive charges to develop on the ground. Negatively charged leaders descend from the cloud and can lead to a much stronger return strike if they drop to within 100 feet of the ground. Most lightning strikes occur at the beginning and end of a thunderstorm. Also, you generally have a brief "safe" period to move after a nearby lightning strike before the ground charges redevelop.

## PROTECTING YOURSELF AGAINST LIGHTNING

In 1990, after a lightning-caused fatality in the summit hut (and a subsequent lawsuit), the hut was retrofitted. It was grounded with wires, and a wood floor was installed to insulate visitors from the ground. Nonetheless, it is still recommended that you do not sit out an electrical storm inside the hut. Instead, if you are caught near the summit in a lightning storm, follow the tips described here to help minimize your chances of being struck and to reduce the risk of sustaining severe injury if you are struck. Once a storm is overhead, it is more important to follow these rules than to try to reach lower ground:

- Get in the lightning position, both to reduce the likelihood of a direct strike and to reduce the seriousness of any injuries you sustain. The National Outdoor Leadership School recommends squatting on the balls of your feet as low as possible and wrapping your arms around your legs. This position minimizes your body's surface area, so there's less chance for a ground current to flow through you. Close your eyes, cover your ears, hold your breath, and keep your feet together to prevent the current from flowing in one foot and out the other.

- Squat on top of an insulated pad or a pile of clothes, if available.

- Place any metal objects—including metal-rimmed eyeglasses—and wet ropes at least 50 feet from you, as they can conduct the current, leading to greater injury. (This probably includes your backpack and most certainly electronic devices.)

- If you are stuck in flattish terrain above treeline, crouch on top of a rock (but not the highest one, of course) that is somewhat elevated or otherwise detached from the rocks underneath it to protect yourself from current flowing through the ground.

- Stay out of shallow caves and away from overhangs.

- If you are part of a larger group, people should be at least 50 feet apart, so multiple people are not injured by a single strike.

- Sit in an area where you are less than 50 feet from, but not directly next to, a much taller object such as a tree.

- Although it's not much of an issue high on the Mount Whitney Trail, avoid individual trees and the tallest trees, instead seeking a larger grove. Also, remember that if a tree is struck, the lightning can discharge through the roots, so stay a good distance away from large trees.

### TREATING LIGHTNING INJURIES

If a member of your party is struck by lightning and stops breathing, immediately begin CPR. CPR is more likely to be successful following a lightning strike than many other injuries, as the electrical shock can stop a person's heart from beating without actually causing much internal damage. Indeed, 80% of strikes are not fatal. (But be prepared to continue CPR or rescue breathing for a long period of time.)

Treat burns by immersing small wounds in cool water (or if available, run cool water over the wound), applying antibiotic ointment to the wound, and covering it with a sterile gauze pad held in place with tape. Plan evacuation and seek medical attention immediately.

## Falling and Knee Problems

A common ailment on the Mount Whitney Trail is knee problems, especially during the steep descent. Don't be tempted to run down the trail for an earlier dinner or because you continued to the summit after your turnaround time: most injuries occur at the end of the day, when you're tired.

The two best ways to avoid knee problems are to walk slowly and to use trekking poles. Walking slowly puts less force on your knee with each step, and using trekking poles takes some weight off your knees. And a bizarre suggestion: Especially if you're wearing a heavy pack, turn around to walk backward down those occasional really tall steps, which significantly reduces the pressure on your knees by employing the stronger muscles of your upper legs. While I can't tell you how much this reduces strain on your knees, it helps me tremendously, and I have converted many friends. Also, if you have had previous knee problems, wear a knee brace.

If you do twist a knee, stop promptly and take anti-inflammatory drugs (such as ibuprofen or naproxen). You may choose to wrap your knee with the elastic bandage in your first aid kit, but don't wrap it too tightly. Then continue (slowly) down the hill, with the help of your group members and perhaps some trekking poles as crutches. (If you twist an ankle, using sports tape is better than using an elastic bandage, as the elastic bandage will provide less stability and support.)

The falls just described might be better called stumbles, and while they can certainly cause serious injury, the injuries are rarely life-threatening. A small number of people experience much more severe falls along the Mount Whitney Trail; indeed, falls are the cause of most deaths along the Mount Whitney Trail. Fatal falls have occurred along the pinnacles near the summit, on the descent of the 99 switchbacks, and even approaching Mirror Lake when a hiker missed the trail. In most cases, altitude sickness, snow, and/or poor weather probably contributed to these unfortunate accidents, but feeling secure as you walk and paying attention to each foot placement will reduce the possibility of a big fall.

## Blisters

Even with broken-in, comfortable shoes, it is easy to get blisters when ascending (and descending) more than 6,000 feet and hiking 21 miles. However, there are many tricks to minimize the severity of blisters and to tackle hot spots as soon as they begin to form. For instance:

- Wear the same shoes you wore on your training hikes (see the section on footwear, page 79).

- Wear well-padded, dry socks. If you are especially prone to sweaty feet, bring along an extra pair of socks to change into halfway up the climb. Most people prefer wool or synthetic socks, which are less prone to abrading your skin. Toe socks are increasingly popular, and proponents praise them for greatly reducing blister occurrence.

- Cover potential hot spots with sports tape, another tape, or moleskin (see the first aid kit section, page 84) either before you start or as soon as you sense a hot spot forming. Use long enough pieces of tape that they don't simply fall off your heel.

*Lightweight Backpacking and Camping* (Beartooth Mountain Press, 2005) has many suggestions for reducing the possibility of injuries, especially blisters. Preventive measures include treating your feet with alcohol for the week before a long hike to toughen your foot and applying Tuf-Skin to your feet before your walk.

If a blister develops, treat it promptly. Some people are content taping over small blisters with a piece of sports tape, but it is often better to apply blister bandages or a piece of moleskin, followed by sports tape. Large blisters are best drained with a sterile pin before patching. Blisters on toes can be very difficult to treat, as taping one toe often causes a blister on the neighboring toe when the tape (or other blister treatment) rubs. Another option is to tape a toe blister with thin tape to minimize rubbing and to proactively tape the neighboring toe.

## Bears—and Smaller Critters

The American black bears' taste for human food makes them a big nuisance in the Sierra. But unless you're fighting them for your food, they are not a danger to humans. Despite their name, black bears come in a variety of colors, including tan and brown. As a result of human visits—and resultant human food—in the high-elevation Sierra Nevada, these smart and highly adaptable creatures have expanded their range upward in these mountains. Historically found predominantly in the midelevation conifer forests of the western Sierra, black bears now roam up to the Sierra Crest and along many of the eastern Sierra drainages, including Lone Pine Creek.

During the 1990s, hikers increasingly returned to trailheads with shreds of stuff sacks and food wrappers. As a result, hikers visiting many parts of the Sierra, including the Mount Whitney Trail, are now required to carry bear-resistant food-storage canisters (see page 92 for more information). The strict food-storage policies are working well: with at least 95% of hikers complying with the regulations, very few people are losing food, and bears are retreating to lower elevations.

When camping, lock your food canister promptly when you finish preparing your meals, and until then always keep your food by your side. This is especially important at Trail Camp, where, although bears are virtually unheard of, you will find quite aggressive marmots and ravens, and they aren't about to relocate to lower elevations. Day hikers do not need to take any precautions other than not ever leaving their food unattended.

Hikers also need to be bear-savvy at the trailhead. Before you leave for your hike, make sure that you remove all food, toiletries, and anything else with an odor from your car and store it in the available food-storage lockers. Guard your food carefully as you pack for your hike—bears can see much better than you can at 2 a.m.

| PREVENTING COMMON TRAIL HAZARDS | |
|---|---|
| Hazard | Prevention |
| Altitude Sickness | • Drink plenty of water and eat food.<br>• Take acclimation hikes. |
| Hypothermia | • Carry all your warm clothes and a space blanket to the top of the mountain. |
| Dehydration | • Drink 5–9 quarts of water during your ascent. |
| Low energy/ fatigue | • Eat small snacks every few hours.<br>• Add electrolyte solution to your water. |
| Lightning | • Do not attempt to summit if there are thunderheads nearby. |
| Knee injuries | • Use trekking poles.<br>• Go slowly. |
| Blisters | • Wear broken-in, sturdy shoes or boots.<br>• Apply sports tape to potential hot spots before the hike.<br>• Stop and patch hot spots as soon as you feel them. |
| Bears | • Store food in a bear-resistant canister. |

# 🌕 *3* 🌕
# Preparations
# and
# Planning

Once you have decided to climb Mount Whitney, it's time to start planning. The Mount Whitney Trail, or more properly, the subset of the trail within the Mount Whitney Zone, is one of only two locations in the Sierra Nevada that impose a quota on day hikers. In addition, like nearly every trailhead in the Sierra, quotas limit the number of backpackers departing from the Whitney Portal trailhead. The implementation of the day-use quota in 1996 was an excellent move: on my first ascent, in mid-September 1995, I reached the summit before 9:30 a.m., and there were already 30 people vying for the best vista points. By noon, there were approximately 200 people crowding the area. So many people led to resource damage and detracted enormously from each person's visit. The number of people on the trail certainly disturbed me, and I avoided the summit for several years. It is still a busy trail, but thanks to the quotas, which limit the number of hikers to 100 day hikers and 60 backpackers per day, there are few enough people on the trail that you actually begin to recognize (and greet) people as the hike progresses. (Beginning in 2008, the day-hike quota included permits obtained by day hikers

*Above:* The view from Trail Camp

ascending the use trail up the North Fork of Lone Pine Creek to the technical routes on Mount Whitney, further decreasing the number of people on the Mount Whitney Trail.) The downside is that hiking Mount Whitney cannot be a spur-of-the-moment decision, as you need to choose whether you want to day hike or backpack, as well as your preferred hiking dates, by March 15, the date the permit lottery closes for the season.

## Day Hike vs. Overnight

Some people enjoy attempting the summit in a single, 21-mile day, while others prefer to spread their ascent over two, three, or more days. While many factors may influence your decision, it usually comes down to whether you want to put in the extra effort required to carry overnight gear and use more vacation days in return for a more relaxing ascent and a backcountry camping experience.

Here are some reasons to day hike:

- You dislike carrying an overnight pack.
- Permits are easier to obtain, especially if you are limited to certain dates.
- You prefer the faster pace possible with only a day pack on your back.
- You have limited vacation days.

And here are some reasons to do an overnight trip:

- You prefer the more leisurely pace associated with backpacking.
- You enjoy spending a night in the middle of the mountains.
- You want the extra night(s) to acclimate at an intermediate elevation before pushing for the summit.
- You know your legs and feet do not wish to travel 21 miles in a single day.

I've summited Mount Whitney and many other peaks, both as long day hikes and as part of a backpacking trip, and the experiences are completely different. On a backpacking trip, the camaraderie of my climbing partners and the time spent together in camp are important parts of the excursion. I tend to spend more time enjoying my surroundings and really appreciate that I am in the middle of an amazing wilderness area. On a long day hike, I focus more on the physical requirements of getting up and down the mountain safely, knowing that I will be exhausted by the end of the day but also keeping in mind that I must make it back to the car by dark. I enjoy the physical and mental challenges that come with pushing myself hard, but there is decidedly less "wilderness experience" in my trip. A backpacking trip along the Mount Whitney Trail merges a bit of both experiences, since summiting a tall peak is still the goal of the trip. But a day hike accentuates the endurance aspects of the hike.

## When to Go

Like most people hiking the Mount Whitney Trail, you probably want to maximize your chances of summiting. This means that you should pick a time of year when the hike requires the least physical and mental exertion and has the lowest likelihood of bad weather. This is a probability game, as you can't shift your summit date to match the weather forecast. In the Sierra Nevada, the absolute best conditions generally exist during July and August. However, we are blessed with a long summer, and most days between June and September are pleasant on the mountain. May temperatures are often warm, but the upper slopes of Mount Whitney will almost always still be snow covered; you should attempt at this time only if you have the equipment and skills to navigate up steep snow slopes. Many October days—and sometimes even those in early November—are still perfect for walking, but the temperatures are cooler, the days are shorter, and there may already be new snow patches in shady corners.

Factors that might influence your preferred summit date include:

- **Snow on the trail:** Your first consideration should be to pick a date after most of the snow has melted—early to mid-July is a safe bet most years. Slogging through residual snow on the trail, especially on the 99 switchbacks above Trail Camp, is very tiring. Your feet slip around with each step, and if the day is warm, you will post-hole (sink into the snow). In addition, you are more likely to get blisters if your feet get wet. Most important, by late afternoon the slope will be in the shadows, and the once-slushy snow can quickly become a dangerous sheet of ice.

- **Thunderstorms:** Most thunderstorms occur in July and August, but they can also occur on any warm day through the summer and fall.

- **Strong winds:** Powerful winds, which are more common in June and September than in midsummer, will sap your energy and can be very disorienting.

- **Temperature:** The warmest days are in mid- to late July.

- **Pacific storms:** Weak Pacific storms are often still blowing through in early June, and they return by early to mid-September. Late spring and early fall storms usually drop little precipitation but are very blustery and cold for 12–24 hours while they pass. Fast-moving September storms take many parties by surprise and result in many rescues.

- **Day length:** As long as you are content to walk up much of the mountain in the dark, this is not a major consideration, but days start getting shorter much more rapidly in mid-August. (I prefer starting day hikes in the dark and enjoying the alpenglow on the peaks once I am already above Mirror Lake.)

- **The moon cycle:** A few days after a full moon is the best time for early-morning walking because the moon will not set until after the sun rises. A few days before a full moon is my favorite time for backpacking because evenings are moonlit. For some people, summiting at dawn on the day of the full moon and simultaneously watching moonset and sunrise is well worth the effort of hiking 10.4 miles (or the shorter distance from your camp) in the dark.

- **Air quality:** Forest fires around the Sierra (and beyond) can result in a perpetual haze during midsummer. The clarity tends to increase following the first small Pacific front to blow through in September.

## Wilderness Permits

The most likely stumbling point during the planning stage is getting a permit to enter the Mount Whitney Zone. (Note: This information pertains only to the Mount Whitney Trail; regulations differ for other trails in the region.)

Permits are required for both day hikes and overnight backpacking trips, and trailhead quotas are in effect May 1–November 1. All permits for both day and overnight trips during the quota period are allocated by lottery. Permit requests may be submitted to the lottery between February 1 and March 15, with outcomes being e-mailed in late March. You may submit up to 15 date choices in a single application. Outside of the quota season, you may simply pick up a first-come, first-serve permit at the Eastern Sierra InterAgency Visitor Center.

To submit a permit request to the lottery, visit tinyurl.com/whitneypermit. To fill in your application, begin by filling out the boxes on the left side of the screen. In the "Looking for" box, select your permit type, either "Day Use" or "Overnight." The correct code is then automatically filled into the "Trail/Zone" box. Next, enter your first choice of date to begin your trip and your party size, and then select "Search." Next, choose "See Details," which leads you to another page where you select "Apply Now." At this point, you must log in with a preexisting account or create a new one. Only after these steps can you begin entering alternate dates. Note that the maximum party size is 15.

After logging in, you reach a page where your first choice of date is filled in. You can now enter up to 14 alternate dates. Do not worry; entering additional dates does not change the likelihood of receiving your first choice; it just increases the chances that you will receive a permit on some date. It is well worth tweaking your schedule for a midweek trip. On a busy Saturday in summer, 1,000 people may apply for the 60 overnight permits and well over 500 for the 100 day-use permits. Meanwhile, on a midweek date, there will be fewer than 200 requests for overnight permits and 75–150 requests for day-use permits, vastly increasing your chances of getting a permit. Finally, add alternate leaders' names, complete the checkout process, and pay the nonrefundable $6 transaction fee. Do not submit multiple applications—the Inyo National Forest staff identifies and removes duplicate applications.

HINT: If you miss the lottery but can arrange your schedule to do a midweek day hike, there is a good chance that there will be unclaimed permits—and they're free. Many days, there are 20 unclaimed permits, but you must be at the Eastern Sierra InterAgency Visitor Center outside Lone Pine by 2 p.m. the day before you wish to hike to take advantage of these permits.

Now you must simply wait until after the lottery to finalize your summer plans. By late March you can log in to your account to determine what date (if any) you have received. Beginning April 1 you must accept (or decline) the permit you have been allocated and pay a $15 per person reservation fee. Any permits you have not confirmed and paid for by April 30 will be canceled; on May 1 all unclaimed permits are released and may be reserved immediately at recreation.gov.

Indeed, despite the intense competition for permits, quite a few permits, especially for day use, become available due to cancellations or last-minute no-shows. On quite a few days midsummer, 25% of the day-use permits initially reserved become available to others. This means that many people, especially those with flexible schedules, will later be able to get a permit (see the hint above).

There are a few quirky rules to the permit process:

- Because permits are not transferable, list alternate leaders on your permit application if you want to make sure that your group can still use the permit if the original leader is unable to go on the trip. I usually list the names of all adults in the group to ensure any of them can use the permit.

- Because your permit is for a single 24-hour period, if you wish to do a moonlight ascent, you must reach the Mount Whitney Zone boundary no earlier than midnight.

- Please make an effort to cancel reservations as soon as you know you won't use them—others will undoubtedly wish to use those permits, and the earlier they can make their plans, the better.

- If you wish to do a longer backpacking trip, you can hike in at a different trailhead, such as Cottonwood Pass, New Army Pass, or Kearsarge Pass and exit via Whitney Portal. See other Wilderness Press books, including *Sierra South, Sequoia & Kings Canyon National Parks,* and *John Muir Trail* for details. For the past few years, obtaining the Trail Crest exit permit required for these itineraries has been exceedingly difficult, but I expect this situation to be modified during the lifetime of this book edition, so check online resources.

The last hurdle to getting your Mount Whitney Trail permit is to pick it up. Permits for the Mount Whitney Trail are issued only by the Eastern Sierra InterAgency Visitor Center, located 2 miles south of the center of Lone Pine, at the southeast corner of the intersection of US 395 and CA 136. Overnight permits must be picked up or confirmed by 10 a.m. on the departure date. Day-hike permits must be picked up or confirmed by 1 p.m. the day *before* the permit date.

You may confirm your permit in person or call the Inyo National Forest Wilderness Permit Reservation Office at 760-873-2483. If you wish to pick up your permit after hours, call the number above and have your permit left in the night box, located in a small kiosk along CA 136; this is a fantastic solution if you will not be in Lone Pine during business hours. Note that permits that cross into Sequoia or Kings Canyon National Parks overnight must be picked up in person—this regulation will not affect those doing an out-and-back trip along the Mount Whitney Trail.

Finally, how do you obtain walk-up permits—those that become available through last-minute cancellations or no-shows? Visit the excellent Inyo National Forest website for a detailed account of the complexities regarding the release of these permits: tinyurl .com/permitwhitney. In brief, permits canceled more than 48 hours in advance are rereleased to recreation.gov, where you can reserve them in advance. Permits canceled less than 48 hours in advance can be obtained in person at the Eastern Sierra InterAgency Visitor Center starting at 11 a.m. the day before your entry date. Day-use no-shows—permits that are unclaimed by 1 p.m. the day before the permit date—are released at 2 p.m. Overnight no-shows are released on the permit date at 11 a.m. Note that there will be many people waiting to take advantage of these permits many hours before they are released, and the wilderness office staff will often conduct a mini lottery to distribute the available permits among the interested hikers.

HINT: To better your chances of getting a Mount Whitney Zone permit:

- Include many possible dates.
- Include midweek options.
- Select a small group size.
- Wait to submit your lottery application until later in February. Before submitting your application, download the PDF titled "Lottery Progress Report" at tinyurl.com/whitneylottery, and select less crowded dates.

## Training

Hiking 21 miles is a major undertaking (especially if you choose to do it in a day), and climbing well over 6,000 feet requires a lot of effort. Long before you start worrying about acclimating to high elevation (page 64), you need to get used to walking long distances up and down hills. In other words, you need to be in relatively good aerobic shape, have toned the needed muscles, and have excellent endurance. You do not need to be fast.

Any aerobic exercise will help you get in shape, but the muscles used extensively for walking up and down hills can only be conditioned by walking up and down hills. If you live somewhere with hills, the best form of training is, unsurprisingly, to take long walks. However, if your surroundings are flatter or you don't have time to hike hills regularly, cities are full of training opportunities: walk up and down staircases in a tall building, walk up and down bleachers in a local stadium, or use a stair machine at a gym. Do not underestimate the descent; this long downhill section catches many people unprepared. Also, knee injuries are more likely if the muscles you need to descend gracefully are not strong.

Testing your endurance ahead of time is important to ensure that you are physically and mentally ready to walk for many hours. If you can do a fast-paced 10- to 12-mile hike in hilly terrain, your physical capabilities are unlikely to limit your success. For many newcomers to hiking (or other endurance sports), the mental game is equally difficult. You need to know how to keep going once you are tired—such as once you've reached your goal but the car is still 10.4 miles away. Successfully finishing training walks and other workouts, even if you are tired or bored, is one good way to know you are ready for Mount Whitney.

The final reason for training hikes is to break in a pair of hiking boots or shoes (see more on footwear on page 79). You are more likely to succeed on summit day if painful feet aren't stopping you.

## ACCLIMATION HIKES

The final stage in your training for Mount Whitney is to get your body acclimated to higher elevations. It is best if you can spend several days hiking at moderate elevations just before attempting Mount Whitney. However, I also recommend that you spend at least one weekend during the previous month hiking above 10,000 feet. Indeed, research has shown that repeated exposure to high elevations can help you prepare for a tall summit, even if it isn't immediately before your climb.

If you live in Northern California, a weekend trip to the Tahoe area, the Tuolumne Meadows section of Yosemite, or anywhere in the Eastern Sierra provides ample hiking options. If you live in Southern California, 11,502-foot San Gorgonio Mountain, 10,834-foot San Jacinto Peak, and 10,064-foot Mount San Antonio (also known as Mount Baldy) are good acclimation hikes.

In addition to acclimation hikes you take over the previous month, it is best to do one or more high-elevation hikes within two days of attempting the mountain, especially if you will be day hiking Mount Whitney. The most easily accessible trailheads near Whitney Portal are Horseshoe Meadows and Onion Valley. Horseshoe Meadows is located 40 minutes southwest of Lone Pine and has good trails to locations such as Cottonwood Lakes (described on page 68), Cottonwood Pass, and Trail Pass (described on the next page). Onion Valley lies west of Independence and is a 40-minute drive north of Lone Pine, with trails leading to Kearsarge Pass (described on page 70), Robinson Lakes, and Golden Trout Lakes. Remember, your goal is to acclimate your body, not to tire your legs or bash your feet. A 1,000- to 2,000-foot climb and a 5- to 8-mile day is all you should do the day before you head up the Mount Whitney Trail—you may indeed choose to do only a portion of one of the following hikes described.

If you are driving from the north, there are a number of other easily accessible trailheads with excellent high-elevation walks between Yosemite and Lone Pine, including walks in the Tioga Pass and Saddlebag Lakes areas just east of Yosemite; Duck Pass Trailhead in Mammoth Lakes; and the South Lake, Sabrina Lake, and North Lake Trailheads in the Bishop area.

A visit to the Ancient Bristlecone Pine Forest in the White Mountains is another alternative where you can drive to quite high elevations and enjoy an easy walk. The 4.5-mile Schulman Grove Trail is at nearly 10,000 feet, and the Patriarch Grove, with a collection of trails all less than 1 mile long, is at a little over 11,000 feet. To reach the Ancient Bristlecone Pine trails, follow CA 168 east 12.9 miles from the CA 168–US 395 junction in Big Pine. Turn left (north) onto White Mountain Road. Schulman Grove and its visitor center are 10 miles along a paved road, while to reach the Patriarch Grove you must continue an additional 12.8 miles along a dirt road.

## HIKE 1

## Cottonwood Pass Trailhead to Trail Pass and Beyond

**Distance:** 7.6 miles out-and-back

**Elevation:** ± 1,000 feet

**Maps:** Tom Harrison *Golden Trout Wilderness Trail;* USGS 7.5-minute *Cirque Peak*

**Overview:** This short walk leads you through exquisite foxtail pine forests as you climb to Trail Pass and then follow the Pacific Crest Trail south beyond Mulkey Pass.

**How to Get There:** From Lone Pine, drive 3.1 miles west along Whitney Portal Road, and then turn left onto Horseshoe Meadows Road. Continue straight approximately 20 miles until you reach the end of the road, the Cottonwood Pass Trailhead.

Looking north across Horseshoe Meadow

Leaving the Cottonwood Pass Trailhead, head west to skirt the northern edge of Horseshoe Meadow. After 0.3 mile, you reach a junction and turn left (south), toward Trail Pass. Now crossing sandy mounds characteristic of open flats in the southern Sierra, you cross a stream and climb slightly into foxtail pine forest. The trail climbs gently as it circles around the head of the smaller Round Valley meadow and then begins switchbacking to Trail Pass. This stretch of trail is through beautiful forest of foxtail pines, whose needles encircle the tips of the branches, giving them the appearance of bottlebrushes. As you climb higher, the trees have ever more character after a lifetime of being bashed by winter winds.

After an additional 1.9 miles and a 600-foot climb, you reach Trail Pass and a junction with the Pacific Crest Trail (PCT). You can now follow the PCT in either direction for as long as you wish. I recommend heading south (left), where you will be treated to sporadic views of the Kern Plateau, with its expansive meadows separated by craggy granite outcrops and perfectly round cinder cones. After 0.8 mile, you reach Mulkey Pass, at which point you will cross another (less well-maintained) trail leading from Horseshoe Meadow. Another 0.6 mile along the PCT leads you up to a collection of granite outcrops dotted with exquisite, weather-beaten trees. This is a good vista and a nice place to have lunch and turn around.

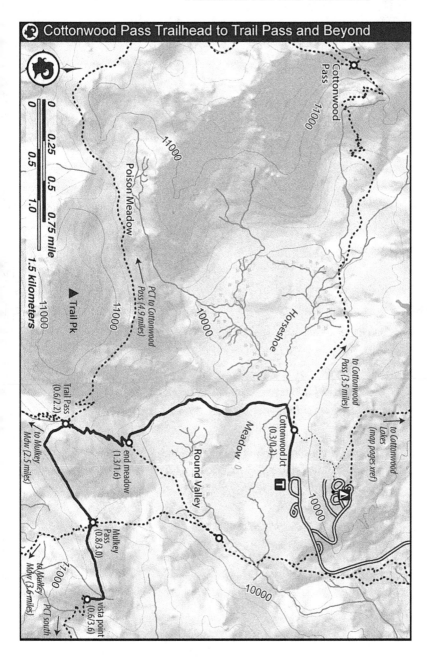

Cottonwood Pass Trailhead to Trail Pass and Beyond

▲ Trail Pk

Cottonwood Pass

Poison Meadow

PCT to Cottonwood Pass (4.9 miles)

Horseshoe

to Cottonwood Pass (3.5 miles)

to Cottonwood Lakes (map pages xref)

Trail Pass (0.6/2.2)

to Mulkey Mdw (2.5 miles)

end meadow (1.3/1.6)

Meadow

Round Valley

Cottonwood Jct (0.3/0.3)

Mulkey Pass (0.8/3.0)

to Mulkey Mdw (3.6 miles)

vista point (0.6/3.6)

PCT south

0   0.25   0.5   0.75 mile
0   0.5   1.0   1.5 kilometers

11000
10000

Walking through the Cottonwood Lakes Basin

## HIKE 2

# Cottonwood Lakes Trailhead to Cottonwood Lakes Basin

**Distance:** 10.0 miles out-and-back to Cottonwood Lakes

**Elevation:** ± 1,100 feet to Cottonwood Lakes

**Maps:** Tom Harrison *Golden Trout Wilderness Trail;* USGS 7.5-minute *Cirque Peak*

**Overview:** This is a lovely trail to walk because it starts high and then climbs just slightly more than 1,000 feet to reach the Cottonwood Lakes, an easy walk through forest and open meadows.

**How to Get There:** From Lone Pine, drive 3.1 miles west along Whitney Portal Road, and then turn left onto Horseshoe Meadows Road. Continue 19 miles until you reach signs pointing you right, toward the trail to Cottonwood Lakes and New Army Pass. Take the right fork, and follow the road, which climbs slightly. Pass a turnoff to the local pack station, and continue to the hikers' parking lot near a pair of campgrounds.

The trailhead is located at the northwestern edge of the parking lot, next to the large information board and toilets. The trail heads west from this point. (Note that some 7.5-minute USGS maps do not accurately portray the configuration of the trailhead or the beginning of this trail.)

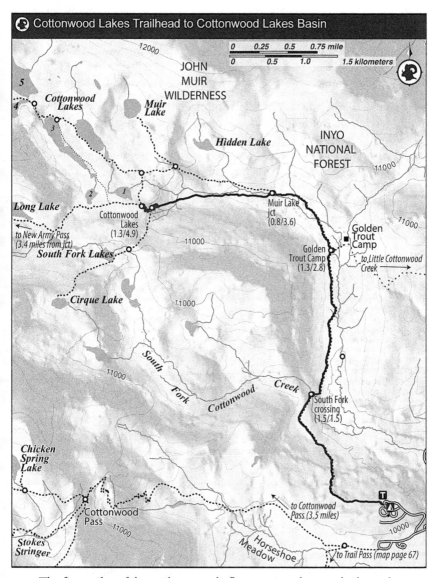

**Cottonwood Lakes Trailhead to Cottonwood Lakes Basin**

The first miles of the trail are nearly flat, passing alternately through stands of lodgepole pine and foxtail pine. The former prefers the flatter, more sheltered terrain, while the foxtails thrive on the more exposed, sandy, dry slopes.

The trail continues through the forest, crosses the South Fork of Cottonwood Creek, and after 2.8 miles reaches an unsigned junction (stay left) for the Golden Trout Camp before a large meadow.

Shortly after the junction for the Golden Trout Camp, you enter John Muir Wilderness. The trail now trends left, passes through another meadow, and begins a steeper climb to the Cottonwood Lakes basin. Soon thereafter, the trail bends nearly due west and follows this trajectory up to and through the Cottonwood Lakes basin.

Stay left at a junction labeled Cottonwood Lakes and right at the junction to the South Fork Lakes (at 11,000 feet). Just beyond a third junction, you reach the first of the Cottonwood Lakes, 2.2 miles after the wilderness boundary. Stop here and enjoy lunch along the banks of this lake. Unlike in most of the High Sierra, trout are native to the Cottonwood Lakes basin. As a result, special fishing regulations are in place to protect the local populations of golden trout. After enjoying the vistas and lake, retrace your route to the car.

**HIKE 3**

## Onion Valley Trailhead Toward Kearsarge Pass

**Distance:** 7.8 miles out-and-back to the plateau below Kearsarge Pass

**Elevation:** ± 2,000 feet

**Maps:** Tom Harrison *Kings Canyon High Country Trail;* USGS 7.5-minute *Kearsarge Peak*

**Overview:** The trail to Kearsarge Pass skirts several lakes that are popular fishing locations and campsites, and then it climbs to timberline for a vista of craggy ridges.

**How to Get There:** From Lone Pine, drive 15 miles north along US 395 to the town of Independence. From the center of Independence take Market Street (Onion Valley Road) 12.5 miles west to its terminus at the Onion Valley Trailhead.

Several trails depart from this large parking area, and the Kearsarge Pass Trail is due west, beyond the toilets and the cluster of bear boxes. From the edge of the parking area, you climb an open slope dotted with dry site shrubs, including sagebrush. Except for a brief interlude beneath tall red firs, the trail continues through similar vegetation for 1.5 miles. Throughout this section, there are views down-canyon to the parking area and beyond.

The trail then skirts above Little Pothole Lake, passing through a few stretches of moister vegetation. After another 0.7 mile, you

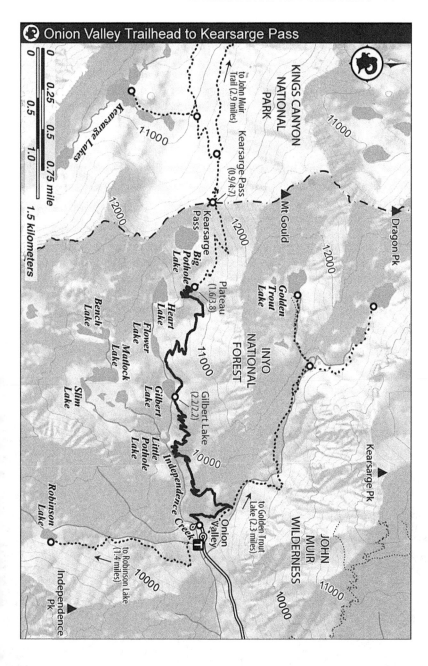

## Onion Valley Trailhead to Kearsarge Pass

KINGS CANYON NATIONAL PARK

Kearsarge Lakes

to John Muir Trail (2.9 miles)

11000

Kearsarge Pass (0.9/4.7)

11000

Mt Gould

Dragon Pk

Kearsarge Pass

12000

12000

Big Pothole Lake

Plateau (1.6/3.8)

Golden Trout Lake

INYO NATIONAL FOREST

Heart Lake

Flower Lake

11000

Bench Lake

Matlock Lake

Gilbert Lake

Gilbert Lake (2.2/2.2)

Slim Lake

Little Pothole Lake

10000

Independence Creek

to Golden Trout Lake (2.3 miles)

Onion Valley

Kearsarge Pk

JOHN MUIR WILDERNESS

Robinson Lake

to Robinson Lake (1.4 miles)

10000

11000

10000

Independence Pk

0

0.25

0.5

0.5

0.75 mile

1.0

1 mile

1.5 kilometers

reach the outlet of Gilbert Lake. The next section of trail passes through a lodgepole pine forest, providing welcome shade.

A short distance beyond Gilbert Lake, you spy nearly hidden Flower Lake, another lovely picnic location, to the left of the trail. The trail now turns away from the drainage, switchbacking up the slope to the north. Approximately 0.9 mile beyond Gilbert Lake, the trail emerges from the forest in a little subalpine flat. Bright pink Sierra primroses are common beneath boulders along this section. Steep talus slopes loom above you as the trail bends left and skirts across a barren slope, leading to a series of tight switchbacks up a slope dotted with stunted whitebark pines. Far below, Heart Lake is visible, accessible via the inlet to Flower Lake.

After 0.8 mile, the grade lessens—a good turnaround spot, as you have now hiked 3.9 miles and climbed 2,000 feet. The trail continues up an increasingly steep slope of sand, gravel, and the occasional boulder to Kearsarge Pass. Switchbacks are visible all the way to the top of the pass, somewhat to the right of the ridge's low point.

View to University Peak from the Kearsarge Pass Trail

# Considerations for Summiting

By the time you reach Whitney Portal, you will have spent many hours planning, training, and assembling your pack of summit gear. This section covers a few more considerations for your trip: group dynamics, pace, and breaks. These are topics to read about before you leave home and to have firmly etched in your mind during your hike. For each of these, I can provide advice but no tangible rules, because how you implement these suggestions is affected by several factors: what pace and break schedule works best for you, as well as your judgment and attitudes about pushing yourself, safety, and group etiquette.

## GROUP DYNAMICS

If you will be ascending Mount Whitney as part of a group, it is important to know each other's expectations before you begin your hike. Realizing partway up the mountain that you have different criteria for turning around, different paces, or simply different goals for the excursion can easily lead to bad feelings and a disappointing hike—not to mention an unsuccessful summit bid. You should discuss these factors thoroughly and honestly with all potential hiking companions.

In my experience, the single greatest source of problems between group members has been neglecting to communicate before reaching the trailhead about levels of experience and goals for the trip. On a trip to 14,375-foot Mount Williamson, someone assured me that he had ample experience at high altitude, only to explain later that he had once been to 10,000 feet. On many trips, people have indicated that they do not mind hiking by themselves if the group should wish to continue faster. But often it turns out that they expressed that opinion only because they wished to join a trip, not because they were actually comfortable hiking alone. On the trip itself, they become resentful if the group walks faster than they do to a meeting point.

However, most trips run smoothly. Usually the group remains together, with the faster hikers taking more time to take in their surroundings and the slower hikers feeling a bit pushed, but not dreadfully so. This works because all group members make small compromises and all have the same time line and agenda in mind.

Also bear in mind that hiking as part of a group will probably cause the entire group to ascend a bit more slowly because each person will be slowest at a different point in time. However, it also tends to

Navigating the handrail section of the 99 switchbacks after the first fall snowstorm

be a lot more fun to have friends with whom to share the experience than to pound up the trail on your own.

Nearly every hiking team—unless you are accompanying a few friends whose pace you know—will be composed of people with different hiking speeds. This requires compromise, patience, and understanding by everyone as you figure out how to accommodate the pace of different group members. Slower hikers may feel bad for holding up the group and therefore agree to turn around even though they would very much like to summit. If the group has agreed in advance to take a certain amount of time for the hike and remain as a group, and you are still within that timetable, the group should stick together. Encourage the slower person to keep going, and take some weight from his/her pack. In contrast, a hiker who cannot keep up the designated pace should realize this and agree to wait in a safe location, alone or with a friend, while others continue to the summit.

If you are part of a particularly large group, people are likely to spread out a little as the hike progresses; pick a buddy in advance, and stick with that person as you hike. A group of more than four or six might even agree to reassemble only at the summit—a big group generally has considerable inertia, as each person is likely to slow down the group at different times.

If the decision is made for the group to split, make sure everyone has agreed on where to reassemble, whether it is at the car or somewhere up the trail. It is very important that everyone knows exactly where and when the meeting location is: many a trip has turned sour when people are waiting at different locations and cannot find their friends.

Do not, however, leave slower people descending on their own. Remember, most accidents occur on the descent, when people are tired and most likely to be suffering from altitude sickness. If a group member is lagging at the end of the day, he or she needs moral and physical support to continue moving slowly and safely to the trailhead.

The following questions will help you discover important concerns (if any) in your group's dynamics. Remember, these are discussions to have long before you begin your hike.

- Do group members think it is necessary to stick together, or can each person go at his or her own pace? As described on page 77, most people have the best endurance when they hike at their preferred pace, neither too fast nor too slow. A good strategy is to allow people to pace themselves but to regroup every mile or two at a predesignated break spot. However, group members should always stick together in the dark or in bad weather.
- What is your turnaround time? Your group should agree on a timetable with a strict turnaround time in advance (see page 112 for likely travel times) and agree to turn around at the time you planned to reach the summit. Because many mountaineering problems arise on the

way down, you should never continue upward after a predetermined turnaround time—just watch the movie *Everest* to see the consequences.

- Under what weather conditions would each person prefer to turn around? People differ in the amount of risk they are willing to tolerate when seeking the summit. No one should feel obliged to continue to the summit if they think conditions are risky or particularly unpleasant. If you are the gung ho person, you should continue to the summit on your own only if it is not late in the day and there are not whiteout conditions.
- Does everyone have the goal of summiting Mount Whitney? If a group member is just coming to take a nice hike, never intending to continue past Trail Camp, he or she should express that in advance because that person will be less inclined to take shorter breaks and forgo photo stops to stick to a timetable.
- Is one person the group leader, calling the shots, or are you hiking as a cooperative, where a consensus must be reached for each decision? The advantage of reaching a group resolution is that everyone's interests have been discussed and no one feels disenfranchised. However, it is unlikely that everyone's preference can be accommodated, and much time can be spent discussing the relative importance of each person's viewpoint. If there is a group leader, that person must listen to everyone's input and attempt to make a fair decision. I generally find that if the group leader is considerate—and that person is one of the most experienced hikers in the group—this leads to faster and often fairer decisions. A good group leader will take into account everyone's needs, even those of less vocal participants who might otherwise be ignored.

As you discuss these considerations, start to develop a plan for your hike. Make sure that everyone has agreed on a starting time, whether from Whitney Portal or a campsite along the trail. Nothing sets a day off to a worse start than pacing around at 4 a.m., waiting for someone who hasn't yet gotten around to filling water bottles, taping heels, and the many other "quick" tasks that expand into a 30-minute (or longer) delay. If you know that you are slow in the morning, get organized the night before and wake up extra early.

## PACE

One key to successfully completing a long hike is determining the pace that allows you to continue for the longest distance before your legs tire. The more practice hikes you take, especially at moderately high elevations, the better you will learn what pace gives you the best endurance. I have learned that I have a range of paces that feel good to my body, but if I have to move more quickly, I need far too many breaks and my legs get tired prematurely. Alternatively, if I hike much more slowly than my normal pace, my legs and breathing never settle into a sustainable rhythm, and both my endurance and motivation are much reduced.

In mountaineering, slower and steady wins the race, and that rule certainly applies to a hike up the Mount Whitney Trail. As you ascend the mountain, keep reminding yourself that, regardless of your speed, having a slower, steady pace is preferable to moving in short, quick bursts interrupted by breaks.

When hiking at high elevation, most people's pace is determined by their lung capacity, and by their legs only toward the end of a long walk. Make a conscious effort to find the right pace to match your breathing—and adjust this pace as you gain elevation. If you find yourself continuously out of breath and needing frequent stops, slow down until your breaths and steps are in a steady, sustainable rhythm. As for those legs, it is difficult to find a pace to overcome tired legs; most people resort to short spurts and quick breaks to compensate for sore muscles. To avoid reaching this state too early, stretch before starting your walk, move slowly for the first mile to let your legs warm up (see below), avoid too many long breaks on the way up, and make sure to eat enough.

Observations and experience have taught me that most people ignore the advice to start out at a slower pace than they are capable of. When you begin your hike, you need to give your muscles a chance to warm up and should therefore go slower than your normal pace for the first 0.5 mile to 1 mile. On this trail, I force myself to move at about 70% of my normal pace until I cross the North Fork of Lone Pine Creek, 0.9 mile from the trailhead. At that point, I speed up a little, but I keep reminding myself that my legs have a long climb ahead and I need to walk slightly more slowly than I would on a shorter hike.

It's also advisable to slow down at high elevation. Between Trail Crest and the summit, much of which is fairly flat, people often attempt to hike along at a faster clip than they can sustain. With few exceptions, they stop every 5 (or fewer) minutes, exhausted and gasping for air. Meanwhile, slightly slower hikers pass them during these breaks and inevitably reach the summit first. A good rule of thumb at high elevation is to keep slowing down until your lungs no longer determine your break schedule. This is, of course, an ideal that is difficult to reach, and even well-paced walkers will need to stop for 30-second quick breathers (see below) at the highest elevations.

## BREAKS

As you ascend Mount Whitney, you will likely take many different sorts of breaks: 30-second breaks to catch your breath, especially on the switchbacks and the last miles to the summit; 5- to 10-minute breaks to eat a snack or patch blisters; and a couple of longer breaks for a more substantial meal. Taking all these types of breaks is necessary, as they allow your body to recharge itself (and allow you to enjoy a quick conversation with your companions). But don't dawdle beyond the suggested times because you rapidly lose precious minutes. In particular, don't let half-minute breathers take up more than that because you don't want your leg muscles to cool down, and you don't want to lose the good walking rhythm that you have established.

You should plan on taking a 5- to 10-minute break every hour, making sure to snack before your body feels low on energy. In addition, most groups will take at least two 20-minute breaks during the ascent, and smart planners will schedule at least an hour for the summit. Indeed, the suggested hiking times on page 112 assume that in addition to quick breathers, you take a 10-minute break for each hour on the trail, such that for a 9-hour ascent, you can take 90 minutes of breaks. If you require additional breaks, your summit times will be greater than those in the table.

If you are the fastest member of a group, remember that the break begins when the last person arrives. Make sure that the stragglers also get 5 minutes to rest their legs and eat. If you are antsy to get going, volunteer to fill water bottles to take your attention off your watch and give the others the downtime they need.

# What to Bring

One must balance safety, comfort, and weight when deciding what to bring on a hike. My basic rule for a day hike is to carry sufficient gear to spend a night (albeit an unpleasant one) in the mountains. This is a tall mountain in a remote wilderness, where you need to be self-reliant. The seemingly abundant hikers on the trail vanish in the late afternoon, and cell phone coverage is much spottier than you might expect.

Most injuries occur late in the day, when you are tired and walking downhill. If your injury means that you need assistance getting off the mountain, know that help will probably not arrive until the following morning. Second, always remember that you are carrying extra clothes for an emergency that could occur on the summit, not just halfway up or down. Temperatures will be much cooler and winds stronger near the summit. Therefore, even if it's a warm and beautiful day, don't be tempted to stash your emergency gear—or first aid kit—halfway up the trail. And don't get too upset with my recommendations when you descend from the summit having never worn more than shorts, a T-shirt, and maybe a light jacket. I often wear none of the warm clothes I carry, but I never ascend to high elevation without them.

I have divided my recommendations on what to pack into four sections: footwear, the 10 essentials, additional gear for a day hike, and additional gear for a backpacking trip. (Backpackers will need to read through all lists.) A checklist of the items in each of the lists is provided on pages 90–91.

## FOOTWEAR

It is difficult to advise others on appropriate hiking footwear, as each person's feet (and ankles and knees) have different needs. The only consensus among the people I've hiked with is to wear comfortable, well-broken-in, but not worn-out shoes on a long hike. These shoes could be full leather hiking boots, lightweight cloth and leather hiking shoes, trail runners, or lightweight running shoes.

Full disclosure: For many years I wore almost exclusively heavy hiking boots. In lighter shoes, I always ended up with very sore feet and felt insecure walking off-trail on talus. I also appreciated being able to walk through creeks or snow without getting wet feet and being able to edge my boot on a snow slope. The downside was that I was more likely to suffer from blisters, which I staved off with multiple layers of sports tape, applied before I started walking. But I quickly learned to stopped trying to convince friends that such boots were the best solution, because they kept coming back from trips—even weeklong off-trail, talus-hopping, rocky Sierra expeditions—complaining that they wished they had worn running shoes. They disliked having to pick up a heavy boot every step of the way, they got bad blisters, and they ended up with sore feet. And then strangely, a few years ago I, for the first time, found trail runners that I actually found comfortable for a full day's walk and now I increasingly wear lighter shoes if I am staying on trails and carrying a day pack or light overnight pack. So while there are still many trails and all off-trail excursions where I prefer boots, my next day hike up Mount Whitney might just be my first in trail runners.

The moral is that making sure you have the right pair of shoes to wear to the summit of Mount Whitney is as important as making sure you're in shape for the hike. These should be shoes that you have worn on many practice hikes, so that you know their shortcomings (if any) and have a plan to combat problems likely to occur.

Here are a few footwear suggestions that should transcend the "lightweight" versus "lots of support" debate.

- Consider bringing more than one pair of footwear. Before my first hike up Mount Whitney, a friend advised me to wear running shoes to Trail Camp and then switch to hiking boots for the upper portion of the trail. This meant that I had to haul hiking boots up the first 6 miles. But the advantage was that I got to wear lightweight, shock-absorbent shoes for the lower, sandier stretches of trail and hiking boots with good ankle support and a tough tread for the rockier sections.
- Choose a pair of shoes with excellent torsional rigidity, which makes it difficult to twist the sole. A rigid sole is one of the features that best protects your ankle from twisting as you walk.
- Don't wear old running shoes with worn-out padding. You will take approximately 60,000 steps on this hike, which will make any foot sore in a worn-out shoe.
- Bring an extra pair of socks. If your feet start to feel beat up on the descent, switch to a clean pair of socks with not-yet-compressed padding to give your feet new life.
- Carefully choose the socks you wear. Toe socks (such as Injinji brand) have helped many people with persistent toe-blister problems. Wool, wool blend, or synthetic socks are generally

preferable to cotton socks because cotton socks retain moisture and more easily lead to blisters.

- Wear a pair of ankle-high gaiters to keep pebbles and sand out of your shoes. Keeping the inside of your shoes clean reduces the likelihood of blisters.

## 10 ESSENTIALS

The oft-mentioned list of 10 essentials covers nearly everything you will need for a summer day hike up the Mount Whitney Trail. The official list includes map, compass, sunglasses and sunscreen, food, water, extra clothes, headlamp or flashlight, first aid kit, fire starter and matches, and knife. To elaborate:

1. **Map:** Simply put, it is dangerous to be in the mountains without a map. Although you're unlikely to get lost along the Mount Whitney Trail, if you wander off the trail (as may happen in the dark) or mistakenly take the wrong trail junction (as many people do at the junction with the John Muir Trail, especially on the descent), you need to determine where you are and how to return to the trail. If you would like to supplement the map on pages 114–115, Tom Harrison's *Mount Whitney Zone* map is a good choice. There are also excellent maps that can be downloaded onto your phone or GPS—just remember that these devices run on batteries and might stop working if dropped. A good choice is Gaia GPS, but search online for the current favorites.

2. **Compass:** You will need a compass if you become disoriented and need to orient your map, identify basic landmarks, and thereby determine the direction to the trail or which direction to follow the trail. (Note that many GPS units do not include a compass.)

3. **Sunglasses and sunscreen:** Sunscreen, sunglasses, and a wide-brimmed hat are musts in the alpine zone. If you don't protect yourself from the sun, you could get more than a nasty burn. Repeated exposure can lead to skin cancer and cataracts. Your sunscreen and sunglasses should be rated to protect you against both UVA and UVB rays, and your sunscreen should be at least SPF 30. To avoid chapped or split lips, bring lip balm that is at least SPF 15. Apply sunscreen at least twice during your long hike up Mount Whitney.

4. **Food:** As discussed in the fuel section on page 47, you will burn thousands of calories on an ascent of Mount Whitney, and it is unlikely that you will consume as many calories as you will expend on your walk. Day hikers should carry enough food to be able to eat a 200- to 500-calorie snack every 1–2 hours. In addition, bring 50% extra food in case something goes wrong or you underestimate your appetite. (Even experienced hikers find that their appetite is unpredictable from day to day, especially at high elevation.) Bring a variety of different foods and foods you expect to find palatable when you are exhausted and at high altitude, where many people find it difficult to eat.

   My snacks tend to consist of energy bars, granola bars, nuts, dried fruit, cookies, jerky, and bread and toppings for lunch. Due to the altitude, many people find it difficult to eat above Trail Camp—so be sure to feed yourself well at lower elevations in case you find food unappealing as you approach the summit. Easily

## RADIATION AT HIGH ELEVATION

The light emitted from the sun includes visible light, heat, and ultraviolet (UV) rays. Of these, UV rays are the highest energy and therefore do the most damage to your body. UV radiation is further divided into UVA, UVB, and UVC. The atmosphere absorbs all of the UVC rays and most of the UVB rays, but little of the UVA; the rest hit you. And they don't just hit you from above: snow reflects 40%–80% of light rays (including UV rays)—and even granite reflects 30% of light—so wearing a hat is only the first layer of protection when traveling in the alpine zone, as the rays bounce back and hit you from below.

Meanwhile, thin cloud cover decreases UV radiation by only 10%, and shade (which is hard to find anyway on the Mount Whitney Trail) decreases UV radiation by as little as 50%. (That's right—you should still be wearing a hat while sitting under a lone tree.) Moreover, UV radiation increases by about 4% for each 1,000-foot increase in elevation: at 10,000 feet, it is 50% greater than at sea level, and at 14,000 feet, it is nearly 80% greater. The only way to avoid it is by covering yourself with clothes, sunscreen, and sunglasses.

digestible foods, such as Gu energy gel, provide your body with a rapidly accessible supply of energy and are generally more appetizing when you are exhausted. I also recommend mixing electrolyte mix into at least some of your water. Full-strength Nuun or Vitalyte (my favorite) are too strong for me. Instead, in a separate bottle I mix a liter at half strength and drink it slowly throughout the day or a cup at a time when I take breaks. Likewise, it is a good idea to eat salty foods.

**HINT:** Make sure that you consume calories regularly, rather than pushing yourself after you begin to feel hungry; it can take your body a long time to regain its energy if you continue upward after you have depleted your muscles' energy stores.

5. **Water:** As described on page 47, staying hydrated is incredibly important in reducing the likelihood that you will suffer from a headache, muscle cramps, or unnecessary fatigue. Hydration also lowers your susceptibility to altitude sickness. Also remember that your body needs you to balance water consumption with food intake; otherwise your electrolyte levels will decrease.

On this hike, 5–9 quarts of water a day should be adequate for most people. A rule of thumb among mountaineers is that if your urine is light yellow, you are well hydrated. This is very useful on an expedition up a remote, snow-covered mountain. Unfortunately, when you (especially if you are a woman) are trying to sneak behind a small boulder on the Mount Whitney Trail and quickly pee into the gray gravel underfoot, you don't necessarily get a good look at your urine. Instead, at each break, check your water supply and make sure that it is disappearing at the rate of a quart every 2–3 miles—or about a pint per hour.

It is also important to pack a hydration system or water bottle that has a 1-gallon capacity. For the first 6 miles, you will cross a stream every few miles, but there is no permanent water from Trail Camp to the summit. This means that for 8.8 miles of the hike, when you are at the highest elevations, you cannot refill your water bottles. Many people leave the summit with empty water bottles—a bad idea.

In addition to carrying enough water up the mountain, you actually need to drink it. During

**HINT:** Before you head up Mount Whitney, determine a water-carrying and -consuming method that works for you. For instance, a bladder-and-tube hydration system lets you drink as you are walking, letting you slowly and steadily consume water throughout your hike. Alternatively, carrying a water bottle lets you efficiently gulp large quantities of water, but you need to be disciplined to stop frequently to drink.

your training and acclimation hikes, determine a system that works for you. I highly recommend a bladder-and-tube hydration system such as the CamelBak. I nearly doubled my water consumption when I switched to this system. Alternatively, a growing constituent of hikers is using water bottles fitted with individual squeeze filters, which purifies the water as they drink. If it's a cool day and you're not inclined to drink much, you may want to set a watch alarm to beep every 5 or 10 minutes to remind yourself to take a few sips.

Lastly, if you plan to treat or filter your water, pack the appropriate device. See page 48 for a description of options.

6. **Extra clothes:** You should carry sufficient clothes to spend a night out on the trail—up to an elevation of 14,505 feet. If you get lost or injure yourself late in the day, a rescue is unlikely until morning. At minimum, bring thermal tops and bottoms; a wool or fleece hat; and a waterproof, wind-resistant jacket. Adding a fleece or puffy top and a pair of polypropylene gloves will greatly increase your comfort if a problem occurs, yet they weigh less than a pound. If you are hiking early or late in the season, when you may encounter snow, throw in an extra pair of socks, as you may end up with wet feet. (If you don't own clothing made from fancy outdoor fabrics, it doesn't mean that you'll be unsafe. Make sure you bring a warm, noncotton top and a pair of noncotton pants.)

7. **Headlamp or flashlight:** Nearly everyone walks part of this trail in the dark and will therefore need a light source. A headlamp is preferable because it allows you to have both hands free. My favorites are light-emitting diode (LED) headlamps, which weigh only a few ounces and run on a triplet of AAA batteries for at least 50 hours—the light gets dimmer with time but never quite gives out. In addition, the dimmer, diffuse light from the LEDs is better for walking than the brighter, more direct light from incandescent bulbs: your pupils remain sufficiently dilated to see the edge of the trail, and irregularities in the trail surface stand out better. Indeed, I prefer half-used batteries for night walks.

HINT: When walking downhill in the dark, I sometimes hold my headlamp at waist level, as I make more shadows that highlight irregularities in the trail when lighting the path at this angle.

8. **First aid kit:** Your first aid kit will most likely be used to prevent and treat blisters, limit an altitude-induced headache, and dull the pain from sore knees. If you sustain a serious injury, it also needs to keep you comfortable and medically stabilized, in case you need to wait to be evacuated.

   A basic first aid kit for a day hike or short backpacking trip should contain:

   - **Tape:** This essential first aid component can be used to prevent or treat blisters, to tape anything in place, and to provide compression. An ideal anti-blister tape stays in place for many days but isn't too thick. I am very fond of simple, thin, cheap sports tape. If I use long pieces, it stays put and doesn't add bulk to my feet. However, many people complain that cheap sports tape rubs off very easily, especially if you have sweaty feet. Some recommend using duct tape, which I dislike because it makes a permanent sticky mess of socks. Other suggestions for thicker, very sticky tapes include Leukotape (available online; also sold as Leukoplast outside the United States).
   - **Anti-inflammatory pain medication:** For mild pain relief and to relieve swelling following an injury, ibuprofen, aspirin, and naproxen are all available over the counter. Acetaminophen is not an anti-inflammatory drug, but it is a very effective painkiller. Of these, ibuprofen and acetaminophen are easier on your stomach. If you take any of these, make sure that you are well hydrated (to avoid kidney damage) and follow the indications on the product or the advice of your physician.
   - **Blister bandages or pads or moleskin:** Examples of blister bandages include Spenco 2nd Skin Blister Pads and Band-Aid Blister Cushions. Blister pads are expensive but highly recommended by people with persistent blister problems: the gel pads keep out dirt and germs while providing cushioning, so your blister won't bother you for the rest of your hike.
   - **Elastic bandage:** With an elastic bandage, you may be able to make slow progress down the trail with a strained or sprained ankle or knee. You can also use sports tape for this purpose.
   - **Sterile gauze or adhesive pads:** These are handy to halt bleeding. There are many inexpensive brands of

## SPECIAL WINTER AND SPRING CONSIDERATIONS

Most of the information in this book assumes that you are embarking on your hike once most of the snow has vanished from the Sierra, but many people visit the mountain off-season each year. If you are not experienced traveling on snow, I strongly recommend that you plan your trip for the mid-June–late-September window, when you will be walking on little to no snow. But also, before ignoring this sidebar, note that there is often snow on the switchbacks between Trail Camp and Trail Crest through the end of June—or later in high snowfall years, so make sure you're prepared for the extra challenge.

If there is snow on the trail, you need to both carry extra gear and—at least as important—rethink your exact timing for crossing snowy slopes. During the spring months, the snow is busily melting during the warm days and then freezes into a solid sheet of ice overnight. Unless you are wearing crampons and heavy hiking boots and are carrying an ice ax (and know how to use it), you do not want to cross snowfields until they have had 30 minutes of morning sun, which will melt the top snow layer enough to kick your foot in effectively. Likewise you do not want to find yourself descending a snowy slope once the afternoon sun has left the slope, as the snow can refreeze very quickly. This means that you cannot begin the ascent above Trail Camp until 6–7 a.m. and must be descending from Trail Crest no later than 4 p.m. On the other hand, by 10 a.m. the snow can become horrendously slushy, and you will instead post-hole—sink deep into the snow—with each step. This is one of the most utterly exhausting ways to climb a steep slope.

Because this is such a popular trail, by June there will likely be a deep rut in the snow where many previous hikers have plodded through, giving you decent protection from a big fall and reducing the risk of post-holing, but it is still more dangerous and more tiring than a "dry" hike. As for extra gear? My first recommendation is to wear heavier footwear (such as sturdy leather boots) with a base that can more readily kick into the snow. You could also bring a pair of trail crampons (such as Microspikes) or true crampons to increase your stability on hard snow or ice. If large stretches of the trail are still snowbound, you should also have an ice ax—and the knowledge of how to self-arrest. Finally, bring a pair of lightweight gloves. I'm a wimp on steep, icy snow and often find myself wanting to use my hands for balance. There is nothing worse than having frigid fingers and trying to avoid touching the snow when you know it makes you more secure.

Finally, a warning: Do not descend straight down the snowfield at the top of the switchbacks. This is a long, steep slope, with boulders often protruding through the snow toward the base. Several people have died descending this way. Stick to the switchbacks that have been routed onto the earlier-melting part of the slope.

adhesive pads to cover wounds. The more expensive Tegaderm adhesive pads are permeable to water vapor and oxygen, but they provide a barrier to microorganisms, making them ideal if you can't reach a doctor within a few hours. Sanitary pads can also be used for this purpose, although they won't breathe.

- **Bandages:** Carry a variety of sizes, including butterfly closures. Band-Aids are great for any small cuts, while Steri-Strips can effectively close a larger wound to reduce bleeding.
- **Antibiotic ointment:** Apply antibiotic ointment (triple-action formulas are best) to a wound before dressing it.
- **Antiseptic wipes:** Use these to clean a wound before applying dressing.
- **Antihistamine:** Carry an over-the-counter antihistamine in case you have an allergic reaction or allergies. If you are severely allergic to something, you may need to carry a prescription-strength remedy, such as an EpiPen.
- **Whistle and signal mirror:** Use these to attract attention to yourself if you are alone when injured.
- **Tweezers:** Use these to remove splinters.
- **Safety pins:** These are useful for fashioning clothing into slings or large bandages. Large, sturdy ones are handy for small repairs, from broken zippers to backpack straps. Zip ties also work well for fixing broken backpacks.
- **Sterile, nonlatex gloves:** Wear these if you are treating an open wound on another person.

- **Small first aid book:** Purchase a pamphlet-sized book at an outdoors store or download one on your phone.

**Other items** you might choose to carry in your first aid kit include:

- Wire splint
- Chemical hand-warmer packets
- Prescription pain medication
- Anti-diarrhea drug, such as loperamide
- Knee brace

9. **Fire starter and matches:** These are important safety items to carry, always living in my backpack. That said, they are of limited use along the Mount Whitney Trail, for it is against U.S. Forest Service regulations to build a fire along the entire length of the trail. Moreover, above Mirror Lake, there is little to nothing to burn—and tugging away at the very slow-growing shrubs and trees would do enormous environmental damage. Be sure to carry sufficient clothing to survive a night at any elevation along the trail, and use your matches only to light your stove.

10. **Knife:** A small pocket knife, especially one with a pair of scissors, is important for cutting first aid supplies—and probably for preparing your lunch.

## DAY-HIKE GEAR

In addition to the 10 essentials, day hikers should carry the following:

- **Day pack:** Any small backpack will work. Some day packs that are covered with gadgets and many small pockets can weigh 4 or more pounds, but they aren't necessary for this hike. Pick a simple one. Some people prefer a hip pack, but make sure you bring one that can accommodate a gallon of water.
- **Water-treatment method:** See page 48 for options.
- **Space blanket:** A space blanket costs less than $5, weighs about 3 ounces, and can help you retain body heat. Bring one to reduce the possibility of hypothermia if you spend an unplanned night on the mountain. I consider this as important as the 10 essentials.
- **Wag Bag:** You will receive one of these human-waste disposal kits free when you pick up your wilderness permit. Although they include a small amount of toilet paper, you may want to bring

extra, together with alcohol-based hand sanitizer. See page 93 for more information.

**Optional items include:**

- **Trekking poles:** Many hikers carry trekking poles. Their advantages include taking weight off your knees, transferring some of the work to your arms, and providing extra balance, thereby minimizing your risk of falling.

- **Camera:** A camera is hardly optional for most people setting out for Mount Whitney, but it's not required for your safety.

- **GPS unit or altimeter:** You might find that the climb passes more quickly (or more slowly) if you can watch yourself making continual progress in distance and elevation. Many people load trail maps onto their GPS unit or smartphone, but these should not substitute for a paper map.

- **SPOT or Personal Locator Beacon (PLB) device:** Long-distance hikers are increasingly carrying an emergency beacon. SPOT devices require a paid subscription and allow the user to transmit both their location and short text messages via satellite to family, friends, and/ or emergency services. PLBs can simply be activated, triggering an immediate emergency response and notification of contacts. PLBs are known to be more reliable but do not allow you to relate details about the emergency situation. Neither is a necessity along the Mount Whitney Trail.

- **Insect repellent:** During June and early July, the section of the trail between Lone Pine Lake and Mirror Lake may be home to swarming mosquitoes. If you march steadily through this area without any breaks, they shouldn't be too bothersome.

## OVERNIGHT GEAR

In addition to the 10 essentials and the day-hike gear, backpackers should carry the items in this section. I provide few details on the different sorts of backpacks, tents, sleeping bags, and stoves, as many books are written on these subjects and much information is available online and at outdoor stores if you are planning to buy new gear for this excursion.

- **Overnight backpack:** Either an internal- or external-frame backpack works well.

*Continued on page 92*

## PACKING CHECKLIST

**Note:** Items in *italics* are optional.

| | Day Hike | Overnight |
|---|---|---|
| ☐ Day pack | • | • |
| ☐ Overnight backpack | | • |
| ☐ Food | • | • |
| ☐ Water bottles/hydration system | • | • |
| **Route-Finding** | | |
| ☐ Map (or GPS) | • | • |
| ☐ Compass | • | • |
| **Sun Protection** | | |
| ☐ Sunglasses | • | • |
| ☐ Sunscreen (SPF 30+) | • | • |
| ☐ Lip balm (SPF 15+) | • | • |
| ☐ Sun hat with ear protection | • | • |
| **Clothes** | | |
| ☐ Shoes | • | • |
| ☐ Wool or synthetic socks | • | • |
| ☐ Fleece or wool hat | • | • |
| ☐ Thermal bottoms | • | • |
| ☐ Thermal tops | • | • |
| ☐ Fleece or puffy top | | • |
| ☐ Rain/wind jacket | • | • |
| ☐ Rain/wind pants | | • |
| ☐ Hiking shirt | • | • |
| ☐ Hiking shorts or pants | • | • |
| ☐ *Gaiters* | • | • |
| ☐ *Extra socks* | • | • |
| ☐ *Gloves* | • | • |
| **First Aid Kit** | | |
| ☐ Tape | • | • |
| ☐ Pain medication | • | • |
| ☐ Moleskin/blister bandages | • | • |
| ☐ Elastic bandage | • | • |

|  | Day Hike | Overnight |
|---|:---:|:---:|
| ☐ Sterile gauze and adhesive pads | • | • |
| ☐ Miscellaneous bandages | • | • |
| ☐ Antibiotic ointment | • | • |
| ☐ Antiseptic wipes | • | • |
| ☐ Antihistamine | • | • |
| ☐ Whistle and signal mirror | • | • |
| ☐ Tweezers | • | • |
| ☐ Safety pins | • | • |
| ☐ Sterile gloves | • | • |
| ☐ First aid book | • | • |

**Miscellaneous**

|  | Day Hike | Overnight |
|---|:---:|:---:|
| ☐ Headlamp | • | • |
| ☐ Fire starter | • | • |
| ☐ Matches | • | • |
| ☐ Knife | • | • |
| ☐ Water treatment | • | • |
| ☐ Space blanket | • | • |
| ☐ Wag Bag and toilet paper | • | • |
| ☐ *Trekking poles* | • | • |
| ☐ *Camera* | • | • |
| ☐ *GPS/Altimeter* | • | • |
| ☐ *Locator beacon* | • | • |
| ☐ *Insect repellent* | • | • |
| ☐ Tent/shelter | | • |
| ☐ Sleeping bag | | • |
| ☐ Ground pad | | • |
| ☐ Stove | | • |
| ☐ Stove fuel | | • |
| ☐ Cooking pot | | • |
| ☐ Eating utensil | | • |
| ☐ Eating vessel | | • |
| ☐ Bear-resistant food-storage canister | | • |
| ☐ Toiletry kit | | • |

*Continued from page 89*

- **Additional clothes:** In addition to the clothes in the 10 essentials list, make sure you have a warm fleece or puffy jacket and a pair of wind or rain pants. During June or September, you might choose to bring a down vest or jacket to make your evening at 12,000 feet more pleasant.
- **Sleeping bag:** In summer, if you are a warm sleeper, a 30°F bag should suffice, while cooler sleepers will prefer a 15°F–20°F bag.
- **Ground pad:** Either a closed-cell foam pad or an inflatable mattress works well.
- **Tent, tarp, or bivvy sack:** If the weather forecast is for clear skies, a tent isn't necessary—although it is a good windbreak and provides extra warmth. Also note that mosquitoes are not much of a problem at Trail Camp but might be pesky at Outpost Camp. Despite what many detractors say, it is perfectly feasible to pitch a non-freestanding tent in the Sierra, even on slabs or shallow soil; you just have to be creative with string and rocks.
- **Stove and fuel:** Most choices will work, but note that fuel canisters and alcohol stoves do not heat water as efficiently as white-gas stoves at high elevation or in the cold.
- **Cooking pot:** Any lightweight camping pot works well. One 2-liter pot works well for groups of one to three, while larger groups might choose to carry a second pot.
- **Bear-resistant food-storage canister:** These canisters are required along the Mount Whitney Trail. Which canisters are allowed changes often, but a quick Web search for "Sierra allowed bear canisters" should tell you the current models. Garcia canisters are the most widely available and can be rented from any Inyo National Forest ranger station, usually for $5 per trip (no reservations necessary). I use the lighter-weight Bearikade canister that can be bought or rented from the manufacturer, Wild Ideas (805-693-0550; wild-ideas.net).
- **Additional food:** In addition to lunch and snacks, be sure to carry hearty breakfasts and dinners. I always start my dinner with a cup of instant soup. My body needs the salt and enjoys the warm liquid.
- **Eating utensils and eating container**
- **A simple toiletry kit:** This should include a toothbrush and toothpaste, personal medications, extra toilet paper, and tampons or sanitary pads, if applicable. Keep it simple because toiletries need to be stored in your bear-resistant canister at night.

## HUMAN WASTE ON THE MOUNT WHITNEY TRAIL

Until the summer of 2007, composting outhouses existed at Outpost Camp and Trail Camp. Unfortunately, the cool, dry climate in the mountains is not conducive to rapid decomposition, and the substantial use each season rapidly overwhelmed the toilets. Barrels of human waste had to be taken out by helicopter. Staff at Inyo National Forest decided that this was not a sustainable solution and began phasing in a "pack out your waste" campaign in 2006.

In 2007 the toilets were removed and their previous locations so well restored that it is difficult to pinpoint where they once stood. (The toilet that once stood at the summit of Mount Whitney saw a similar end in 2006 for this reason.) When you pick up your permit, you'll be given a Wag Bag to pack out human waste. The kits consist of two concentric bags: the inner bag has an absorbent powder that both deodorizes and helps break down solid waste, and the outer bag zips closed for easy transport. They do a remarkable job of not reeking. There is obviously a big yuck factor associated with depositing your human waste into a small plastic bag and carrying it, but without toilets it really is the only practical solution in such a high-use area. Use the bag, put your toilet paper inside, douse your hands with an alcohol-based hand sanitizer or wash with water away from a stream, and continue your walk.

There are specially marked bins at Whitney Portal in which to deposit your used bags. A side benefit of removing the toilets is that backpackers are now less inclined to camp only at Outpost Camp and Trail Camp. There are plenty of other beautiful little sandy shelves between Mirror Lake and Trail Camp that are suddenly being used again. The biggest downside of no toilets: it is very hard to find privacy along the trail to do your business.

## Getting There

The small town of Lone Pine is located at the eastern base of the Sierra, 13 linear miles east of the summit of Mount Whitney. If you're coming from out of town to hike Mount Whitney, Lone Pine or one of the nearby campgrounds will be your base. Whitney Portal, where the Mount Whitney Trail begins, is 13 miles along a paved road west of Lone Pine. Lone Pine is located along

US 395 in the Owens Valley in southeastern California; by car, it is approximately 4 hours north of Los Angeles, 7 hours southeast of San Francisco, 4 hours west of Las Vegas, and 5 hours south of Reno, Nevada.

The following directions are written from the major airports. Please consult a map for additional information.

**From Los Angeles International Airport in western Los Angeles:** As you exit the airport, head east on I-105. After 1.5 miles, exit and drive north on I-405, toward Santa Monica. Continue 29 miles to the junction between I-5 and CA 14. Drive north on CA 14 for 118 miles to the US 395 junction near Ridgecrest. Continue north on US 395 for 65 miles to Lone Pine. Total distance: 214 miles.

**From Ontario International Airport in eastern Los Angeles:** Exit the airport onto I-10, and head east, toward San Bernardino. After 2.5 miles, turn onto I-15, and continue 30 miles to the US 395 junction. Take US 395 North 164 miles to Lone Pine. Total distance: 197 miles.

**From the San Francisco International Airport:** Head south on US 101 for 7 miles and then turn east onto CA 92, toward Hayward. After 14 miles, you reach I-880 and head north 3.5 miles. Now turn onto I-238 south, which you follow 3 miles until it merges with I-580. Head east on I-580, continuing 29 miles, until you are east of Altamont Pass at the junction between I-580 and I-205.

You then have the choice of heading north, via Yosemite National Park, or heading south down the Central Valley. Both routes require a similar amount of time from this junction.

If you head north, take I-205 for 13.5 miles to I-5. Drive north on I-5 for 2 miles, and then turn east onto CA 120. After 6 miles, turn north onto CA 99. Continue 2 miles, and then continue east on CA 120. Follow CA 120 through Oakdale, the Sierra foothills, and Yosemite National Park to Lee Vining, a distance of 155 miles. From Lee Vining (east of Yosemite), drive south on US 395 for 121 miles. The only words of warning: CA 120 through Yosemite National Park is usually closed from late October until at least Memorial Day weekend, and you'll have to pay the National Park Service entrance fee to drive through Yosemite. Total distance: 357 miles.

If you choose to head south, continue an additional 17 miles on I-580 to I-5, and follow I-5 south 167 miles. Take Exit 278, turn east onto CA 46, and follow it 25 miles to CA 99. Head 20 miles south on

Downtown Lone Pine

CA 99 to Bakersfield. In Bakersfield, turn east onto CA 58, and follow it 58 miles across Tehachapi Pass to the CA 14 junction. Head 44 miles north on CA 14, and then merge with US 395, heading north an additional 65 miles to Lone Pine. Total distance: 455 miles.

**From Las Vegas International Airport:** Exit the airport onto I-215 westbound and follow it 2 miles. Then turn south onto I-15, following it just 1.4 miles, exiting west (right) onto NV 160. Follow NV 160 for 82 miles, until just north of Pahrump, Nevada. Turn west (left) onto Bell Vista Avenue and go 26 miles to CA 190. Now turn west (left) onto CA 190 and follow it 116 miles, through Death Valley National Park. Continue straight ahead on CA 136, where CA 190 turns south, for an additional 18 miles. You are now on US 395; follow it just 2 miles north to Lone Pine. Total distance: 221 miles.

**From Reno-Tahoe International Airport:** Drive south on US 395 for 257 miles.

**Once you reach Lone Pine, here are directions for getting to Whitney Portal:** The Mount Whitney Trailhead lies 13 miles west of Lone Pine (US 395 doubles as Lone Pine's Main Street). Turn west at the only stoplight in town onto Whitney Portal Road. The road winds through the Alabama Hills and eventually climbs steeply to Whitney Portal. (See pages 97 and 98 for maps of Whitney Portal.)

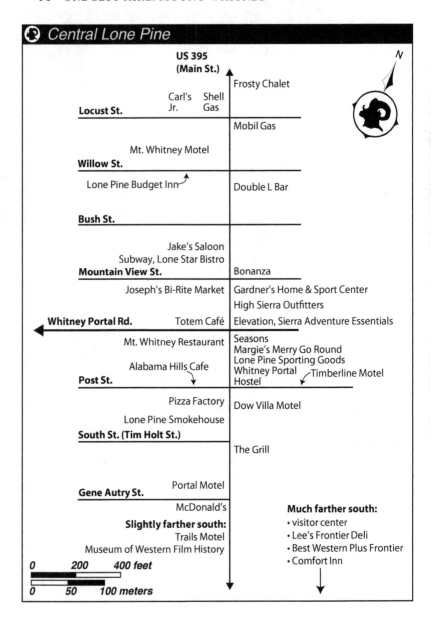

## Central Lone Pine

US 395 (Main St.)

N

Frosty Chalet

Carl's Jr.    Shell Gas

**Locust St.**

Mobil Gas

Mt. Whitney Motel

**Willow St.**

Lone Pine Budget Inn

Double L Bar

**Bush St.**

Jake's Saloon
Subway, Lone Star Bistro
**Mountain View St.**

Bonanza

Joseph's Bi-Rite Market

Gardner's Home & Sport Center

High Sierra Outfitters

**Whitney Portal Rd.**    Totem Café

Elevation, Sierra Adventure Essentials

Mt. Whitney Restaurant

Seasons
Margie's Merry Go Round
Lone Pine Sporting Goods
Whitney Portal Hostel    Timberline Motel

Alabama Hills Cafe

**Post St.**

Pizza Factory

Dow Villa Motel

Lone Pine Smokehouse

**South St. (Tim Holt St.)**

The Grill

Portal Motel

**Gene Autry St.**

McDonald's

**Much farther south:**
• visitor center
• Lee's Frontier Deli
• Best Western Plus Frontier
• Comfort Inn

**Slightly farther south:**
Trails Motel
Museum of Western Film History

0    200    400 feet

0    50    100 meters

# Lone Pine and Whitney Portal

People began to inhabit Lone Pine around 1863 to provide supplies for the nearby mining towns. By the 1920s Lone Pine had become a hub for the film industry, especially for Westerns. Since then, 400-plus films have been shot in the surrounding Alabama Hills.

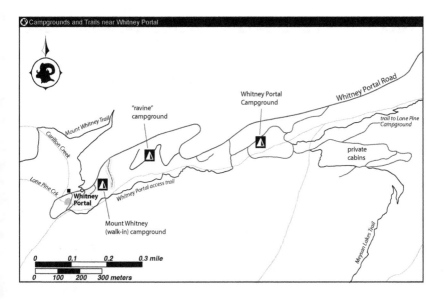

Campgrounds and Trails near Whitney Portal

HINT: Keep your gear close to you—especially in the dark. The bears know the layout of Whitney Portal very well and have good night vision. They are often lurking in the shadows, watching hikers organizing for predawn starts. If you leave your pack—full of your food for your hike—unattended as you use the toilet, you just might discover it gone on your return.

The declining popularity of Westerns in the 1950s brought fewer film crews to Lone Pine, but even today, commercials and films are regularly shot in the Owens Valley, where Lone Pine is located. The desert foreground flanked by steep mountains is an undeniably dramatic setting. (To learn more about Lone Pine's movie history, visit the Museum of Western Film History; see page 144 for details.)

Whitney Portal, the trailhead for Mount Whitney, was established following the construction of the Whitney Portal Road between 1933 and 1935. The private cabins near the Whitney Portal campground were erected beginning in 1934, and the Whitney Portal Store was built in 1935. The store, a mainstay of the Whitney experience that serves food off the grill, has been run by its current owners, Doug and Earlene Thompson, since 1987. It is also packed with last-minute essentials you need for your hike, including snacks, ponchos, and maps. Many people doing the Mount Whitney Trail as a three-day trip plan to return to Whitney Portal before 11 a.m. to get a plate of pancake. (Yes, that's *pancake,* not *pancakes.* It is so large that almost no one can finish it alone.) Also, grab a copy of the book *Mount Whitney: Mountain Lore from the Whitney Store*

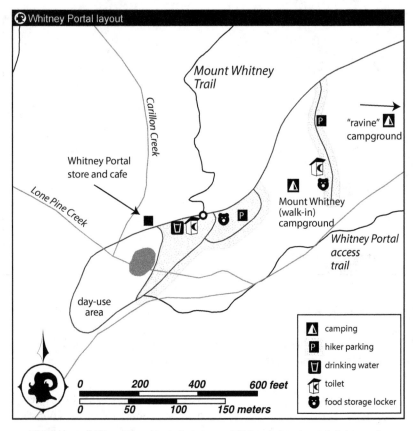

Whitney Portal layout

*Mount Whitney Trail*

Carillon Creek

"ravine" campground

Whitney Portal store and cafe

Lone Pine Creek

Mount Whithey (walk-in) campground

*Whitney Portal access trail*

day-use area

| | |
|---|---|
| camping | |
| hiker parking | |
| drinking water | |
| toilet | |
| food storage locker | |

| 0 | 200 | 400 | 600 feet |
|---|---|---|---|
| 0 | 50 | 100 | 150 meters |

The layout of Whitney Portal is really quite straightforward—when it is light out. As you're trying to get organized to start hiking at 2 a.m., it helps to know in advance where to find bear boxes, the water tap, toilets, and the trailhead.

(Westwind Publishing Company, 2003) for more stories and tidbits about Whitney's history.

## Lodging and Camping

Due to the popularity of the Owens Valley and Whitney region of the Sierra Nevada as tourist destinations, there are many nearby lodging and camping choices. Most of the independently owned motels in Lone Pine have similar prices. The newly opened and economical Whitney Portal Hostel is run by the Thompsons, the Whitney Portal Store owners. At the hostel are five public showers ($7) open 24 hours a day. Campgrounds exist on both public land and on land owned by the Los Angeles Department of Water and Power. Staying at the higher-elevation campgrounds is recommended during the summer: temperatures are more pleasant, and camping up high will help your body acclimate. For additional information about lodging in Lone Pine, visit the Lone Pine Chamber of Commerce website at lonepinechamber.org.

## LONE PINE HOTELS AND MOTELS

### Best Western Plus Frontier Motel
1008 S. Main St.  |  760-876-5571 or 800-528-1234
bestwesterncalifornia.com/hotels/best-western-plus-frontier-motel

### Comfort Inn
1920 S. Main St.  |  760-876-8700
comfortinnlonepine.com

### Dow Villa Motel & Hotel
310 S. Main St.  |  760-876-5521 or 800-824-9317
dowvillamotel.com

### Lone Pine Budget Inn & Motel
138 W. Willow St.  |  760-876-5655 or 877-283-4381
lonepinebudgetinn.com

### Mt. Whitney Motel
305 N. Main St.  |  760-876-4207 or 800-845-2362
mtwhitneymotel.com

### Portal Motel
425 S. Main St.  |  760-876-5930 or 800-531-7054
portalmotel.com

### Timberline Motel
215 E. Post St.  |  760-264-4401
facebook.com/pages/Timberline-Motel/361214993925714

### Trails Motel
633 S. Main St.  |  760-876-5555 or 800-862-7020
trailsmotel.com

### Whitney Portal Hostel and Hotel
238 S. Main St.  |  760-876-0030
mountwhitneyportal.com

## RV FACILITIES

### Boulder Creek RV Resort
2550 S. Main St. (US 395, 4 miles south of Lone Pine)
760-876-4243 or 800-648-8965  |  bouldercreekrvresort.com

## OTHER ACCOMMODATIONS

### De La Cour Ranch
5000 Horseshoe Meadows Road (9 miles west of town, south of Whitney Portal Road)
760-264-3213 | delacour-ranch.com

### Mt. Williamson Motel and Base Camp
515 S. Edwards St., Independence (15 miles north of Lone Pine along US 395)
760-878-2121 | mtwilliamsonmotel.com

## CAMPING

*Note:* None of these camping options offer RV hookups.

Inyo National Forest: For campgrounds in this section that accept reservations, you can reserve online by searching for the campsite name at recreation.gov or by visiting www.fs.usda.gov/activity /inyo/recreation/camping-cabins and following the links provided under the individual campground names.

- *Mount Whitney Trailhead*
  Located adjacent to the Whitney Portal parking area, this campground has 25 first-come, first-serve walk-in sites. One-night stay only. *Price:* $12/site. *Amenities:* Water, pit toilets. An additional 12 walk-in campsites are located in the ravine below the overflow parking area—the trail to access the so-called Mount Whitney "ravine" campground is easily missed. See the map on page 97 for its location.

- *Whitney Portal and Whitney Portal Group*
  Located 1 mile east of Whitney Portal, near the Meysan Lakes Trailhead on Whitney Portal Road, this campsite has 43 standard sites and 3 group sites. The group sites and 60% of the standard sites can be reserved; the others are first come, first served. Camping at Whitney Portal the night before your hike will help your body acclimate, so this is a good spot to choose if you plan to day hike the mountain. *Price:* $21/standard campsite; $73/group site. *Amenities:* Water, pit toilets.

- *Lone Pine and Lone Pine Group*
  Located off Whitney Portal Road: From Lone Pine, drive 6.5 miles west on Whitney Portal Road, and look for the campground on the south side of the road. There are 43 campsites and 1 group site here. The group site and 60% of the standard sites can be reserved; the others are first come, first served. *Price:* $20/standard site; $63/group site. *Amenities:* Water, pit toilets.

PREPARATIONS AND PLANNING  **101**

- *Other Inyo National Forest Campgrounds*
  The Cottonwood Lakes Trailhead and Cottonwood Pass Trailhead campgrounds, located a 40-minute drive southwest of Lone Pine in the Horseshoe Meadows area, are good alternatives. These $6 first-come, first-serve campgrounds are at nearly 10,000 feet and near a number of trails (see page 64), making them a good base for acclimating. The reservable Onion Valley Campground ($18) is located west of Independence at an elevation of 9,000 feet—and it's the location of the Kearsarge Pass Trailhead, a good training hike. The Inyo National Forest campground website lists many additional options that are a bit farther afield.

## Bureau of Land Management

- *Tuttle Creek*
  Located off Horseshoe Meadows Road: From Lone Pine, drive 3.5 miles west on Whitney Portal Road, and turn left (south) to drive 1.5 miles on Horseshoe Meadows Road. From there, follow signs to the campground. Tuttle Creek has 85 first-come, first-serve campsites. *Price:* $5/site. *Amenities:* Pit toilets, water.

## Los Angeles Department of Water and Power

- *Portagee Joe*
  Located off Whitney Portal Road: From Lone Pine, drive less than 1 mile west on Whitney Portal Road, and turn left (south) to drive 0.1 mile on Tuttle Creek Road. This campground has 15 first-come, first-serve sites. *Price:* $10/site. *Amenities:* Water, pit toilets.

- *Diaz Lake County Park*
  Located on the west side of US 395, 2 miles south of Lone Pine, this campground has 200 sites, which you can reserve two weeks in advance by calling 760-876-5656. *Price:* $14/site. *Amenities:* Water, flush toilets.

# Restaurants

Lone Pine has plenty of restaurants, from fast food to pricier but very tasty steak houses. A selection of menu items is provided. Note that only summer hours are listed.

## Alabama Hills Cafe and Bakery
111 W. Post St.  |  760-876-4675
*Hours:* Wednesday–Monday, 6 a.m.–2 p.m. *Menu:* Freshly baked bread, breakfast, burgers, sandwiches, pasta, and steak

### Bonanza Mexican Restaurant
104 N. Main St. | 760-876-4768
*Hours:* Monday–Friday, 11 a.m.–8 p.m.; Saturday–Sunday,
8 a.m.–8 p.m. *Menu:* Full selection of Mexican food

### Carl's Jr.
401 N. Main St. | 760-876-1035
*Hours:* Saturday–Thursday, 6:30 a.m.–10 p.m.; Friday, 6:30 a.m.–
11 p.m. *Menu:* Burgers and other fast food

### Frosty Chalet
532 N. Main St. | 760-920-4940
*Hours:* Daily, 11 a.m.–8 p.m. *Menu:* Burgers, hot dogs, ice
cream, shakes, and other drive-through classics

### The Grill
446 S. Main St. | 760-876-4240
*Hours:* Daily, 7 a.m.–9 p.m. *Menu:* Full selection of classic—and
tasty—diner food

### Lee's Frontier Liquor and Deli
1900 S. Main St. (next to the Chevron) | 760-876-5844
*Hours:* Daily, 4 a.m.–8 p.m. *Menu:* Deli sandwiches, soup, and
fried chicken

### Lone Pine Smokehouse
325 S. Main St. | 760-876-4433
*Hours:* Daily, noon–8 p.m. *Menu:* Barbecue and sandwiches

### Lone Star Bistro
107 N. Main St. | 760-876-1111
*Hours:* Daily, 6 a.m.–10 p.m. *Menu:* Deli sandwiches, soups,
coffee, and ice cream

### Margie's Merry Go Round
212 S. Main St. | 760-876-4115
*Hours:* Daily, 5–10 p.m. *Menu:* Steaks, seafood, and Asian food

### McDonald's
601 S. Main St. | 760-876-4355 or 760-876-4366
*Hours:* Daily, 5 a.m.–10 p.m. *Menu:* Burgers and other fast food

### Mt. Whitney Restaurant
227 S. Main St. | 760-876-5751
*Hours:* Daily, 6:30 a.m.–9 p.m. *Menu:* Breakfast, lunch, and dinner; specializes in a diverse selection of burgers, including
venison, buffalo, and ostrich

**Pizza Factory**
301 S. Main St.  |  760-876-4707
*Hours:* Sunday–Thursday, 11 a.m.–9 p.m.; Friday–Saturday,
11 a.m.–10 p.m. *Menu:* Pizza and salad

**Seasons Restaurant**
206 S. Main St.  |  760-876-8927
*Hours:* Daily, 5–9 p.m. *Menu:* Steak and seafood

**Subway**
101 N. Main St.  |  760-876-1860
*Hours:* Daily, 7 a.m.–10 p.m. *Menu:* Sandwiches

**Totem Café**
131 S. Main St.  |  760-876-1120
*Hours:* Daily, 7 a.m.–9:30 p.m. *Menu:* Breakfast, sandwiches,
burgers, steak, and seafood

**Whitney Portal Store**
Located at Whitney Portal  |  760-876-0030
*Hours:* June and September, 8 a.m.–8 p.m.; July and August,
7 a.m.–9 p.m. *Menu:* Breakfast, giant pancakes, burgers, sandwiches, and more off the grill

# Outdoor Equipment Shops

**Elevation, Sierra Adventure Essentials**
150 S. Main St.  |  760-876-4560  |  sierraelevation.com
*Note:* This is Lone Pine's only well-outfitted mountaineering
shop, with equipment rentals available, even after hours (the
owner's number is on the store door).

**Gardner's Home & Sport Center**
(True Value Hardware)
104 S. Main St.  |  760-876-4208

**High Sierra Outfitters**
130 S. Main St.  |  760-876-9994

**Lone Pine Sporting Goods**
220 S. Main St.  |  760-876-5365

# 4
## Hiking
## Mount Whitney

## How Long It Takes

The amount of time you require to reach the summit is determined by your pace and the time you spend taking breaks. The formula is different for each person, and the optimal solution for you can only be determined through practice. When you are on training hikes, try different walking paces on different days to learn how your lungs and legs feel under different conditions. Over time, you will discover a pace that feels right.

There are two tricks to converting that knowledge into a successful hike up Mount Whitney. First, take enough training hikes so that you know how your lungs and legs feel when you are walking at a pace you can sustain for many hours. Don't focus on your speed because it can be wildly different on different trails, but you'll have the same pair of legs and lungs. Second, on a very long hike, such as this one, force yourself to go about 80% of your good pace because

*Opposite and above:* Trailside Meadow

you have a long way to go. I have hiked with many very fit, gung ho hikers who sped past me during the first hours of the walk but ran out of reserves long before the top and were unable to summit.

## DAY-HIKE TIMING

| Suggested Start Times for Day Hikes | | | |
|---|---|---|---|
| Month | 7-Hour Ascent (13-hour round-trip) | 9-Hour Ascent (16-hour round-trip) | 11-Hour Ascent (19-hour round-trip) |
| June and July | 6:45 a.m. | 3:45 a.m. | 12:45 a.m. |
| August | 6:15 a.m. | 3:15 a.m. | 12:15 a.m. |
| September | 5:30 a.m. | 2:30 a.m. | 11:30 p.m. |

The hike up the Mount Whitney Trail to the summit of 14,505-foot Mount Whitney is approximately 10.4 miles, with nearly 6,500 feet of altitude gain. First-time day hikers should expect the ascent to take 9–11 hours, especially because you are at high elevation. A quite fast time to the summit is 5–6 hours.

Most people will find the descent faster, likely taking you between half as long to two-thirds as long. (The fastest round-trip time on the Mount Whitney Trail is just over 3 hours and 20 minutes.)

To determine when to leave, work backward from the latest acceptable return time—plan to be back at Whitney Portal an hour before dark. Going uphill in the dark isn't a problem, but at the end of a long day, it is simply too easy to trip walking downhill in the dark. It is also more difficult to illuminate the trail while walking downhill than uphill. In addition, if an accident does occur, you don't want it to be in the dark, when help will probably not arrive until the following morning.

The math to determine your trip time is as follows:

- Plan to take 9–11 hours to ascend. If this is your first time on such a long hike, it is, of course, difficult to estimate exactly how long it will take you. Based on conversations with a variety of first-timers, I've determined that most people climbing the mountain for the first time take 9 hours, and about a quarter of hikers need at least 11 hours. (These estimates include 10-minute breaks each hour. If you anticipate taking longer breaks on your ascent, give yourself extra time.)
- Budget an hour on the summit.
- Plan to take 5–7 hours to descend.

- Plan to return an hour before dark. In June and July, it gets dark around 8:45 p.m., in August it gets dark around 8:15 p.m., and by mid-September, it is dark at 7:30 p.m.

When planning your start time, be conservative. I recommend leaving no later than 6 a.m., even if you expect to ascend quickly. The calculations described here do not take into account thunderstorm activity, which would mean you'd need to be off the summit by noon (thus requiring an earlier departure time). If you leave too early, the worst that happens is that you get to take a longer summit break or get back to Lone Pine for an earlier dinner. See the hike timetable on pages 112–113 for more details.

## BACKPACKING TIMING

If you will be backpacking, your first day will be shorter in distance, elevation gain, and time than if you plan to do Whitney in a day, but it is nonetheless a tough hike. The distance to either Outpost Camp (3.8 miles) or Trail Camp (6.15 miles) is unlikely to be the limiting factor. Instead, it is the relentless elevation gain: the trail goes straight up, and you gain approximately 2,000 feet if you stay at Outpost Camp, or 3,700 feet if you stay at Trail Camp. An average hiker will require 4 hours to reach Outpost Camp and nearly 7 hours to reach Trail Camp. Between the trailhead and Mirror Lake (a 4.2-mile stretch), the trail is very hot midday, so it is best to start hiking by 8 a.m. and get the early miles under your belt before lunch. Arriving at your campsite early gives you time to relax and enjoy your surroundings.

### Budgeting Your Time

Your choice of campsite (see next section) will determine the length of your approach hike as well as the time required to summit Mount Whitney the next day. A rule of thumb is that it takes an hour to backpack 2 miles on flat ground, and you add an hour for each thousand feet of elevation gain. In effect, to reach Trail Camp, it takes:

$$6.15 \textbf{ miles} \div 2 = \textbf{3.05 hours}$$
$$+ \ 3,700 \textbf{ feet} \div 1,000 = \textbf{3.70 hours}$$
$$\textbf{Total one-way time} = \textbf{6.75 hours}$$

This time takes into account 10-minute breaks each hour but not lengthy lunches. Using this formula, the amount of time required to reach each of the suggested campsites is included in the table below. Excepting those wishing to bivvy on or near the summit, there is plenty of daylight to reach these campsites. Once you reach camp, expect to spend 2 hours setting up camp, cooking, and eating dinner. Before retiring for the night, make sure you have an agreed-upon wake-up time. Organize your summit pack, fill your water bottles, and prepack your lunch (and then store it inside your bear canister). Mornings are chilly at high elevation, and it is easy to forget something when it is dark and you are half asleep, so do as many of these tasks as possible the day before.

Although your summit day does not require as much of a predawn start as it does for those day hiking from Whitney Portal, you should still set out from Trail Camp between 6 and 7 a.m. and from Outpost Camp between 4:30 and 6 a.m.—and perhaps an hour earlier if you want to take your time or need to return to Whitney Portal in the afternoon. The table below indicates how long you will likely require to summit. Remember to budget an extra hour to pack up camp once you have completed the summit, and keep in mind that

## CAMPSITE LOCATIONS

| Description | Distance from Whitney Portal (miles) | |
|---|---|---|
| **Lone Pine Lake:** Sites beneath scattered lodgepole pine cover, especially on the ridge north of Lone Pine Lake | 2.9 | |
| **Outpost Camp:** Large camping area beneath foxtail pines southwest of the creek crossing | 3.8 | |
| A few small sites beneath foxtail pines above **Mirror Lake**; lovely sites but far from water | 4.5 | |
| Small, sandy sites among slabs on open knob above **Trailside Meadow** | 5.2 | |
| Many small, sandy sites among slabs along the trail a short distance before **Trail Camp** | 5.8 | |
| **Trail Camp:** Many sites in sandy flats among slabs on both sides of trail; additional, more isolated sites if you continue south from Trail Camp | 6.1 | |
| Several small, very exposed, sandy bivvy sites among talus in the vicinity of the **John Muir Trail junction,** mostly just below the **Mount Whitney Trail** | 8.5 | |
| **Mount Whitney summit:** Various bivvy sites on the summit plateau | 10.4 | |

NAD83 is the datum used on most current topo maps. WGS84, the datum for GPS units, is nearly identical. Note that most printed USGS topos still use the NAD27 datum.

it will take you about half to two-thirds as long to descend as it did to ascend. Plan to be back at the trailhead an hour before dark.

## Where to Camp

Along the Mount Whitney Trail, backpackers have a limited selection of campsites, as there is relatively little flat real estate in the vicinity of water (see the table below). The largest sites are at Outpost Camp (at 10,370 feet) and Trail Camp (at 12,040 feet), and these are obviously well used. During summer, close to 50 people camp at Trail Camp each night. Fortunately, the underlying substrate is sandy, so these sites are not dusty like heavily used camps at lower elevations. Without the attraction of the solar toilets, more parties are opting for other smaller sites, but Outpost Camp and Trail Camp still attract the most people.

A few small sites exist beneath foxtail pines on the slope above Mirror Lake (at 10,840 feet), although the closest water is at least a 10-minute walk back down the trail to Mirror Lake. (Camping

| Time from Whitney Portal (hours) | Time to Summit (hours) | Elevation (feet) | Approximate UTM Coordinates (NAD83) |
|---|---|---|---|
| 3.1 | 7 | 10,010 | 11S 388132E 4048552N |
| 4 | 6.5 | 10,370 | 11S 387371E 4048057N |
| 4.7 | 6 | 10,840 | 11S 387045E 4047831N |
| 5.6 | 5.3 | 11,430 | 11S 386612E 4047627N |
| 6.5 | 4.7 | 11,900 | 11S 385921E 4047181N |
| 6.75 | 4.5 | 12,040 | 11S 385536E 4047156N |
| 9.5 | 1.75 | 13,460 | 11S 384267E 4047015N |
| 11.75 | N/A | 14,505 | 11S 384393E 4048899N |

Stands of foxtail pines between Outpost Camp and Mirror Lake

## LEAVE NO TRACE

Even in a location as busy as the Mount Whitney Trail, we need to remember that, as proclaimed by the Wilderness Act of 1964, man is only a visitor in lands protected as wilderness and may not dominate the landscape. Following the seven Leave No Trace principles is an easy way to ensure you are minimizing your impact. Indeed if you look carefully at the regulations on your Mount Whitney permit, you will realize that the specific requirements—from human waste management to the prohibition of campfires to campsite selection and food storage—are all necessary if visitors are going to "Leave No Trace," as embodied by these principles:

- Plan ahead and prepare.
- Travel and camp on durable surfaces.
- Dispose of waste properly.
- Leave what you find.
- Minimize campfire impacts.
- Respect wildlife.
- Be considerate of other visitors.

© 1999 by the Leave No Trace Center for Outdoor Ethics: lnt.org.

is prohibited along the banks of Mirror Lake.) Between Trailside Meadow (camping prohibited) and Trail Camp, there are scattered sites (between 11,430 and 11,900 feet) in sandy patches between granite slabs, mostly less than a 5-minute walk from water. If you wish to camp farther from the trail, there are sites near the shores of Consultation Lake (11,680 feet) or south of Trail Camp.

Here are some things to consider in determining the best site for you:

- **Regulations:** Regulations detailed on your wilderness permit indicate that you should camp 100 feet from the trail or water sources, and you should never camp on vegetation, including meadows. The fragile subalpine and alpine meadows can take years to recover from disturbance, so please take the ecology into account if you wander off the trail in search of a campsite. Camp only on sandy flats and previously used sites.

- **Elevation:** If you camp higher, you put yourself at greater risk for altitude sickness, but you will also have a more leisurely summit day. Few people coming from low elevation sleep well at 12,000 feet, but the advantages of an alpine perch may outweigh the headache and lack of appetite the night before. Nonetheless, if you have never camped above 10,000 feet and have not spent the previous day (or days) doing an acclimation hike, I recommend camping at Outpost Camp: you will probably sleep better and will therefore better enjoy your hike to the summit.

Sign on the summit declaring the completion of the Mount Whitney Trail

The bivvy sites near the John Muir Trail junction (13,460 feet) or on the summit of Mount Whitney offer the most spectacular alpine views, but they are also cold, windy, and high enough that you are guaranteed to feel the elevation.

- **On trail or off trail:** There are advantages and disadvantages to both. If you camp at the designated sites, you won't have to detour from the trail to search for a flat spot of sand and won't risk having difficulty finding the trail for your predawn start. On the other hand, you'll have more privacy off trail.

- **Distance from the summit:** Your summit day will be shorter if you select a higher campsite. However, do not force yourself to camp high if you are concerned that you will spend the night feeling sick due to the altitude—this will decrease your chances of summiting the next day.

- **Crowds:** The large number of tent sites at Outpost Camp and Trail Camp mean that you will have many neighbors at these locations. However, the sites are picturesque with very easy access to water, and plenty are on flat ground.

- **Early morning noise:** Because many day hikers are leaving the trailhead not long after midnight, they start traipsing past Outpost Camp by 3 a.m. and Trail Camp before 5 a.m. If you don't plan on rising so early, select a campsite far from the trail to reduce the noise and disruption of all those headlamps.

## HIKE TIMETABLE AND ITINERARY

| Location | GPS (UTM) Coordinates (NAD 83) | Elevation (feet) | Distance (miles) |
|---|---|---|---|
| **Whitney Portal Parking Lot** | 11S 389057E 4049762N | 8,330 | |
| **North Fork of Lone Pine Creek** | 11S 388593E 4049760N | 8,720 | 0.9 (0.9) |
| **Lone Pine Lake Junction** | 11S 388117E 4048454N | 10,010 | 1.9 (2.8) |
| **Outpost Camp** | 11S 387364E 4048086N | 10,370 | 1.0 (3.8) |
| **Mirror Lake** | 11S 387104E 4048011N | 10,670 | 0.4 (4.2) |
| **Trailside Meadow** | 11S 386539E 4047555N | 11,420 | 0.9 (5.1) |
| **Trail Camp** | 11S 385536E 4047156N | 12,040 | 1.0 (6.1) |
| **Trail Crest** | 11S 384420E 4046765N | 13,670 | 2.2 (8.3) |
| **"End of Pinnacles"** | 11S 384361E 4048065N | 13,860 | 1.1 (9.4) |
| **Mount Whitney Summit** | 11S 384393E 4048899N | 14,505 | 1.0 (10.4) |

Figures in parentheses indicate cumulative information. Elevation gain is often greater than the increase in altitude, due to slight undulations on the trail. Due to those undulations, you also have about 320 feet of *uphill* on the *descent*.

## The Hike Itself

The table below divides the hike into nine sections and includes necessary statistics for each part—UTM coordinates, distance, elevation gain, and estimated timing. The suggested time itinerary is provided for 7-, 9-, and 11-hour ascents. The amount of time needed takes into account distance, elevation gain, and altitude (it assumes you will go more slowly the higher you get). While rest breaks are not explicitly indicated, this timetable allows for 10-minute rest breaks each hour. In each case, the point-to-point and cumulative information is provided (in parentheses). The elevation gain numbers include the extra ups and downs of the trail itself, so don't be confused when you see that the total climb is greater than the 6,175-foot elevation difference between Whitney Portal and the summit of Mount Whitney.

HINT: Take your time getting started: slow and steady is the mantra for success on this hike. Give your legs at least 15 minutes to warm up before speeding up to full pace—your leg muscles will thank you later.

| Elevation Gain (feet) | Timing for 11-Hour Ascent | Timing for 9-Hour Ascent | Timing for 7-Hour Ascent |
|---|---|---|---|
| 390 (390) | 0:35 (0:35) | 0:30 (0:30) | 0:25 (0:25) |
| +1,300, -10 (1,690) | 1:45 (2:20) | 1:30 (2:00) | 1:05 (1:30) |
| +380, -20 (2,070) | 0:40 (3:00) | 0:30 (2:30) | 0:25 (1:55) |
| 300 (2,370) | 0:30 (3:30) | 0:20 (2:50) | 0:15 (2:10) |
| 690 (3,060) | 1:00 (4:30) | 0:50 (3:40) | 0:40 (2:50) |
| 680 (3,740) | 1:00 (5:30) | 0:50 (4:30) | 0:40 (3:30) |
| 1,630 (5,370) | 3:00 (8:30) | 2:30 (7:00) | 2:00 (5:30) |
| +480, -290 (5,850) | 1:15 (9:45) | 1:00 (8:00) | 0:45 (6:15) |
| 650 (6,500) | 1:15 (11:00) | 1:00 (9:00) | 0:45 (7:00) |

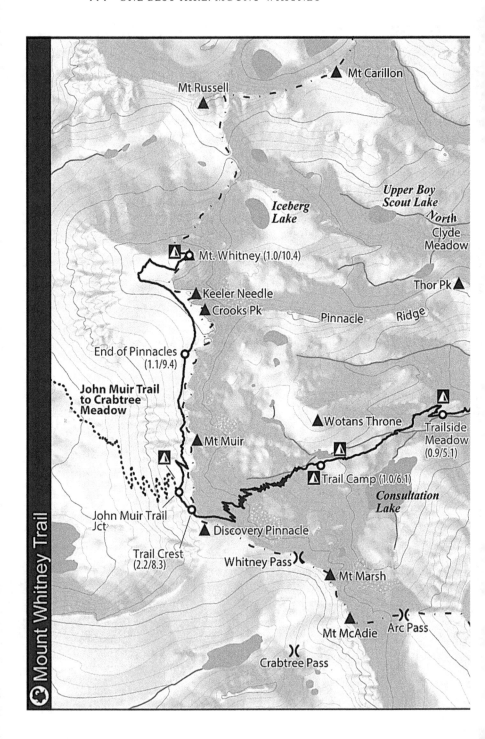

Mount Whitney Trail

Mt Carillon

Mt Russell

Upper Boy Scout Lake

Iceberg Lake

North Clyde Meadow

Mt. Whitney (1.0/10.4)

Thor Pk

Keeler Needle

Crooks Pk

Pinnacle Ridge

End of Pinnacles (1.1/9.4)

John Muir Trail to Crabtree Meadow

Wotans Throne

Trailside Meadow (0.9/5.1)

Mt Muir

Trail Camp (1.0/6.1)

Consultation Lake

John Muir Trail Jct

Trail Crest (2.2/8.3)

Discovery Pinnacle

Whitney Pass

Mt Marsh

Mt McAdie

Arc Pass

Crabtree Pass

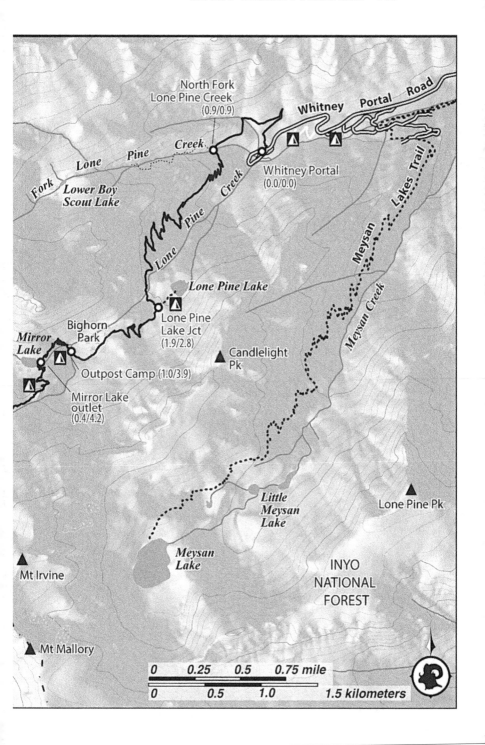

North Fork
Lone Pine Creek
(0.9/0.9)

Whitney Portal Road

Lone Pine Creek

Fork

Lower Boy
Scout Lake

Whitney Portal
(0.0/0.0)

Lone Pine Creek

Lone Pine Lake

Lone Pine
Lake Jct
(1.9/2.8)

Bighorn
Park

Mirror
Lake

Candlelight
Pk

Meysan Lakes Trail

Meysan Creek

Outpost Camp (1.0/3.9)

Mirror Lake
outlet
(0.4/4.2)

Little
Meysan
Lake

Lone Pine Pk

Meysan
Lake

INYO
NATIONAL
FOREST

Mt Irvine

Mt Mallory

0      0.25      0.5      0.75 mile

0          0.5          1.0          1.5 kilometers

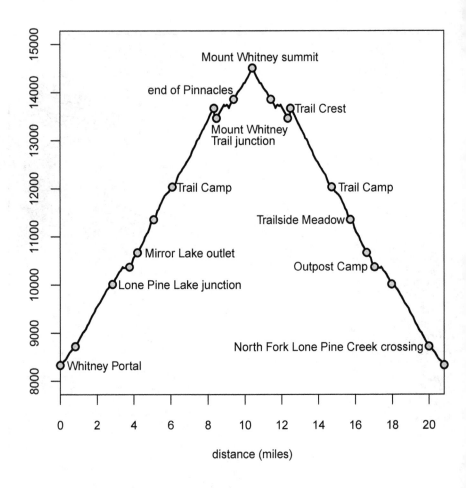

SECTION

**1**

# Parking Lot to the North Fork of Lone Pine Creek

Distance . . . . . . . . . . . . . . . . . 0.9 mile

Leaving the parking lot, head north to the sign pointing to the trailhead; you will pass large information plaques and a handy scale to weigh your pack. The sandy trail begins by heading north, with a couple of quick switchbacks. After crossing a small creek, you emerge onto a dry, sandy slope. After about 0.3 mile, you complete an east-trending switchback and begin a long, westward traverse along the south side of the canyon. Climbing gently, you cross this open slope, which is dotted with drought-tolerant shrubs

**HINT:** Your feet may start to develop blisters along this long stretch of switchbacks. If you feel rubbing, stop promptly to apply blister bandages or sports tape. Stopping for 5 minutes now will save you time later.

The first view after leaving Whitney Portal: Thor Peak, Crooks Peak, and Keeler Needle

and sports an understory of colorful flowers in spring and early summer. Along the way, you cross several small trickles, which might make for short sections of a muddy trail. Nearby, watch for patches of rose thickets to the side of the trail. In the distance is a collection of pinnacles—the Sierra Crest just south of Mount Whitney. Some distance below are the tips of the pine and fir trees growing in the Whitney Portal parking lot. Just before you cross the North Fork of Lone Pine Creek, a sign points right (northwest) to the use trail that hikers and climbers take to access the east face of Mount Whitney and the Mountaineers Route—not your goal today. You stay on the main trail, crossing the creek on large boulders or possibly getting your feet wet during the highest flows. On the return trip, you'll appreciate the soft sand underfoot along this stretch of trail.

## SECTION 2

# North Fork of Lone Pine Creek to the Lone Pine Lake Junction

Distance . . . . . . . . . 1.9 miles (2.8 miles total)

After crossing the North Fork of Lone Pine Creek, sidle around to the head of the canyon, and climb a long series of switchbacks. They are well graded, and the trail is sandy with few protruding

Lone Pine Lake

rocks; if you're doing the one-day hike, this is straightforward walking in the dark. The slope begins under a tree cover of Jeffrey pines and white fir and then emerges onto a drier slope of chaparral plants. Higher still, some of the larger shrubs disappear, and the slope is covered with a variety of short shrubs and flowers. Near the end of this climb, the trail veers toward Lone Pine Creek and passes vegetation that requires moister soils—these plants tend to have bigger, thinner leaves. Because this entire stretch of trail is on a single slope with no stream crossings and no junctions, it can feel rather endless; if it is light out, focus on the changes in vegetation and the changing view down-canyon to remind yourself that you are indeed making progress. Just past one open patch with a small meadow and a cluster of lodgepole pines, you reach the Lone Pine Creek crossing. A series of raised logs allows you to traverse the broad crossing easily, although during the highest flows you may get wet while approaching these logs. Beyond the stream, you switchback briefly up through lodgepole pine forest and promptly reach the signed Lone Pine Lake junction. Heading left (east) leads to the round lake, perched on the edge of the long drop-off to Whitney Portal. The Mount Whitney Trail continues up to the right (southwest).

HINT: The table below indicates easy locations to refill water bottles along the trail. As long as you are carrying a water purification device, there is no need to carry much water until you reach Trail Camp; you can refill your bottles every 1–2 miles.

| Location | Distance from Whitney Portal (miles) |
|---|---|
| North Fork of Lone Pine Creek | 0.9 |
| Lone Pine Creek crossing | 2.7 |
| Outpost Camp | 3.8 |
| Mirror Lake | 4.2 |
| Trailside Meadow | 5.1 |
| Crossing Above Trailside Meadow | 5.6 |
| Trail Camp | 6.1 |
| Spring Above Trail Camp (seasonal) | 6.3 |

**SECTION**

**3**

# Lone Pine Lake Junction to Outpost Camp

Distance . . . . . . . . . . . 1.0 mile (3.8 miles total)

At the beginning of this section, you enter a sandy flat and pass the sign declaring your entry into the Mount Whitney Zone—beyond this point all hikers require a permit. To the south is a blocky talus field flanked by tall, steep cliffs; this is the north face of what is unofficially called Candlelight Peak. Sandier sections mark an area

Stately rock walls above the Lone Pine Lake junction

Bighorn Park

with recurrent rockfall and avalanches. Shortly, a series of switchbacks begins, taking you in and out of scattered foxtail pine cover as you ascend. In places, elegant rock walls support the trail. Along this stretch, scattered stands of foxtail pines replace the denser lodgepole forests. At the end of the climb, the trail drops slightly into Bighorn Park, a marshy meadow beneath towering cliffs. To your right (north) is the meandering Lone Pine Creek, and to your left are little wet crevices with an enticing collection of small, wetland plants that are rare elsewhere along this trail. At the west end of the meadow is Outpost Camp, the first of the two large campsites along the Mount Whitney Trail. There are a few small campsites northeast of the trail, but most people choose to pitch their tents southwest of the trail, beneath tall foxtail pines. South of these campsites, Lone Pine Creek cascades over a cliff face in a tumbling waterfall.

HINT: Be sure to stop and have a snack every 1–2 hours. Your body's performance may decrease for the next many hours if you keep exerting yourself once your muscles start to deplete their glycogen stores.

**SECTION 4**

## Outpost Camp to Mirror Lake

Distance . . . . . . . . . . .0.4 mile (4.2 miles total)

For this short stretch of trail, you diverge from Lone Pine Creek and head slightly north to climb gravelly switchbacks along the north wall of the canyon. These south-facing slopes are dry and hot and correspondingly covered with plant species that do well with very little water. The shrub bush chinquapin, with prickly fruit and golden-backed leaves, dominates much of this section, with various colorful flowers growing underfoot. Shortly, the trail intersects the stream drainage and you climb briefly on slabs alongside the creek before crossing the Mirror Lake outlet on large blocks of rock. To the north is Thor Peak, the large mountain whose steep cliff faces extend all the way to the shores of Mirror Lake. Note that camping is prohibited at Mirror Lake.

HINT: If it is still dark as you approach Outpost Camp—and later Trail Camp—please remember your headlamp etiquette: shine your light at the ground (and keep your voice low) to avoid disturbing people who are still asleep.

Mirror Lake

The waterfall at the back of Outpost Camp

## SECTION 5

# Mirror Lake to Trailside Meadow

Distance . . . . . . . . . 0.9 mile (5.1 miles total)

Above Mirror Lake, the trail climbs steeply via tight switchbacks that cut through a granite bluff—pay attention to make sure you don't lose the trail here. There are a few small campsites tucked in sandy flats along this climb, but if you choose to use them, you must carry water up from Mirror Lake, about 0.2 mile below. You reach the top of a small granite ridge and then turn southwest to rejoin the main Lone Pine Creek drainage. Through this section, the views down to Lone Pine Lake and the Owens Valley are exquisite, especially when early morning light illuminates the granite walls. You are now walking through a landscape of slabs—in places the trail winds along small sandy passageways, and elsewhere you walk atop the slabs themselves. You'll now pass the last trees, mostly foxtail pines, along with a few stunted whitebark and lodgepole pines, and enter the alpine zone. A collection of shrubs, herbs, and grasses grow from the base of boulders and out of cracks in the slab. The tall granite walls of the surrounding peaks are suddenly much closer. To the north, Mirror Lake is already far below you. The trail mostly follows the crest of a small granite ridge, occasionally dropping into sandy flats that formed along fractures in the rock. Some distance later, you reach Trailside Meadow, an important waypoint: it is almost exactly the halfway point in terms of both distance and elevation. The small meadow, covered with shooting stars, is a refreshing place to take a short break, but camping here is prohibited.

HINT: Although the path you are following appears flat compared to the surrounding slopes, the trail continues upward at a good clip—take it easy and pace yourself.

Gazing down on Mirror Lake and Thor Peak

**SECTION 6**

# Trailside Meadow to Trail Camp

Distance . . . . . . . . . . .1.0 mile (6.1 miles total)

Above Trailside Meadow, the trail makes a couple of small switch-backs as it climbs out of the drainage and back up onto slabs. If you look at a topo map, you'll see that you have been following the nose of a small ridge radiating east from Wotans Throne. But shortly you begin a traverse across a steep slope leading back into the creek drainage. You cross Lone Pine Creek, which is particularly flower-lined at this location, and proceed up more granite slabs toward

Climbing slabs above Trailside Meadow

Consultation Lake with Arc Pass and Mount McAdie behind

Trail Camp. Imperceptibly step-by-step, the trail is becoming rockier; you are increasingly stepping over protruding rocks or walking on cobble and have to pay more attention to your footing. To the south, the skyline from left to right is Mount Irvine, appropriately shaped Arc Pass, Mount McAdie, and Mount Marsh, a small summit just beyond Mount McAdie. Consultation Lake lies below Arc Pass. If you wish to camp at Consultation Lake, there are many small use trails that cross the granite slabs; choose any of them once upstream of Trailside Meadow.

Along the last 0.3 mile to Trail Camp, there are many camping options, with water from Lone Pine Creek just a short distance away. Trail Camp itself is a wonderfully scenic campsite and therefore often a zoo of people and tents. There are ample tent sites for everyone, although you can expect to hear the noise of and see the lights from other backpackers and day hikers long before first light. Since there are no longer toilets tethering you to this specific location, if you want more privacy, search for alternate campsites a bit farther south, or select one of the campsites before you reach Trail Camp.

HINT: Make sure you have refilled your water bottles before you leave Trail Camp. From Trail Camp, you have nearly 9 miles of hiking before you return to water.

**SECTION 7**

# Trail Camp to Trail Crest

Distance . . . . . . . . . 2.2 miles (8.3 miles total)

HINT: Many people find it easier to ascend a long slope like this if they can mentally tick off little bits of it as they go. Some possibilities:
- Count switchbacks.
- Carry an altimeter or GPS that tells you the elevation.
- Watch the peaks to the north become ever more prominent.
- Or my bizarre favorite when I'm tired: count steps. I just count to 1,000 steps over and over again. It keeps my mind focused and I go faster and farther.

No one denies that this is a tough stretch of the trail. You are already at 12,000 feet and face a 1,600-foot slope with a relentless set of approximately 99 switchbacks—some short, some long, and, luckily, all well graded. These switchbacks lead up a long talus slope via a route that avoids both cliff bands and a large snowfield that can hug the western side of the slope well into the summer. The trail is well constructed and the footing is mostly straightforward, but like the terrain, the trail becomes increasingly rocky—there are

The Whitney crest from Trail Camp: Mount Whitney is the summit farthest to the right.

Ascending the stretch of switchbacks blasted into a steep cliff face

small rocks underfoot, and the tips of embedded boulders must be stepped over. About a third of the way up, you intersect a prominent cliff band where the trail has been blasted into rock. Snow and ice can persist here throughout the summer, so a handrail has been installed for safety. Take a moment to gaze down the steep slab of rock extending below the trail and look up at the colorful and jointed rock above the trail. Above this section, the meager vegetation becomes even sparser. See the section on natural history (pages 12–29) to identify some of the plants here.

As you take breathers, stop to look at the mountains. The higher you climb, the more peaks come into view. Mount Muir, with a sharp summit and tall, steep east arête, is the peak nearly due west of Trail Camp, and it dominates the view as you ascend the switchbacks. North of Mount Muir is the long ridge of pinnacles ending with the flat-topped Mount Whitney. Mount Whitney is visible from the lowest switchbacks, but then not again until you are nearly at Trail Crest; Keeler Needle, the next summit south, blocks Mount Whitney from your view. Farther north is notably steep Mount Russell, and to its east is the talus field that leads to the summit of Mount Carillon. The last few switchbacks are longer, and after one final westward traverse, you reach Trail Crest and cross to the west side of the Sierra Crest.

## SECTION 8

## Trail Crest to "End of Pinnacles"

Distance . . . . . . . . . 1.1 miles (9.4 miles total)

HINT: The John Muir Trail, which descends the western slope of Mount Whitney, is more pronounced than the Mount Whitney Trail at the junction west of Trail Crest. Be sure to take the correct (right, north-heading) branch.

The last miles of the trail to the summit of Mount Whitney traverse the slope just west of the crest in Sequoia National Park, crossing talus fields and winding among jagged pinnacles. From Trail Crest, you descend briefly but steeply, skirting past a few rock towers and enjoying the view down to the Hitchcock Lakes and up to Mount Hitchcock. Almost immediately, you reach the junction with the John Muir Trail, where you head right (north). From here to the summit of Mount Whitney, the Mount Whitney Trail and the John Muir Trail follow the same path. You may see backpacks stashed around this junction, as backpackers arriving from the west generally choose to carry only minimal gear to the summit. Beyond the junction, you cross a talus field with a few bivvy sites, some of which are nearly on the Sierra Crest.

At about 13,800 feet, the trail levels off and enters a maze of pinnacles. The slope here has a scalloped appearance due to the many

*Continued on page 133*

The welcome sign at Trail Crest

The trail weaves among the pinnacles as it passes Mount Muir.

## WHERE CAN I FIND PRIVACY?

The lack of toilets along the Mount Whitney Trail (see "Human Waste on the Mount Whitney Trail" on page 93) means that there is nowhere with a privacy screen to use the toilet. Along the lower reaches of the trail, there are trees and it is not too cumbersome (or dangerous) to duck off the trail to do your business. In the vicinity of Trail Camp, my recommendation is to walk some distance away from the main camping area and water sources and find a large boulder to squat behind.

From then on, until you are on the broad summit—with its good supply of large boulders—there really are no good locations to disappear from the ubiquitous hikers. All I can recommend is that you take care of your business quickly and realize that everyone else is facing the same predicament and will do their best to look the other way. I've heard that some women avoid drinking water so they don't have to urinate—this is a terrible idea, greatly increasing your risk of ailments on your ascent and decreasing the chance of summiting.

## CLIMBING MOUNT MUIR

The steep, exposed summit blocks of Mount Muir make this a Class 3 climb, indicating scrambling that requires hands and the possibility of falling as much as 20 feet should you slip. However, if you are comfortable with this, the view of Mount Whitney's summit and the 99 switchbacks are both excellent—and you'll likely have the small summit to yourself. To reach Mount Muir (only 300 feet away), head east on the small use trail and climb loose talus until just below the crest. To your left is a steep rock face. Climb a blocky crack to a 2-foot-wide ledge, and then traverse a few feet to the right into a small gully. Above and left is a 10-foot, blank, low-angle sloping slab, at the top of which are handholds in a small crack. Climb out of the gully onto the slab, which you cross from right to left. Once you are across this, continue up and then right, scrambling between large blocks of rock until you reach a small platform below the summit block. Still on the south side of the summit, climb this last face to the top. Note that after the talus section, this entire description encompasses only 50 feet of elevation gain.

Mount Muir, viewed from the north on the final switchbacks up Mount Whitney

*Continued from page 130*

avalanche chutes that transect it. The sharp ridges of pinnacles mark the boundary between two avalanche chutes. Between pinnacles, you have open views to the west; in the distance are the dark, jagged Kaweah peaks, while granite slopes dominate the foreground. You repeatedly pass narrow notches, with jaw-dropping views straight down to the east—watch your footing carefully near there, for the trail is narrow and the drops are very steep. Near the beginning of this traverse, you may note some rock cairns and well-trod use trails that leave the Mount Whitney Trail in the direction of 14,012-foot Mount Muir, a few hundred feet east.

**HINT:** Along this stretch, you are at nearly 14,000 feet. Try to walk slowly so that you don't need to stop more than once every 15 minutes. Just keep thinking, "breathe-step-breathe-step" or even take two breaths per step—just try hard to find that slow and steady pace that lets you keep going.

SECTION
9

## "End of Pinnacles" to Mount Whitney Summit

Distance . . . . . . . . . 1.0 mile (10.4 miles total)

Leaving the pinnacles behind, you are just 1.0 mile from the summit. Before you is a large, barren talus field. Large boulders are embedded in sand, with ever smaller numbers of alpine gold and sky pilot growing in sheltered crevices. The trail mimics the surrounding terrain; it is still mostly sandy, but there are also boulders embedded in the trail that require larger steps up—not a welcome proposition at this altitude. Traverse the western face of Crooks Peak (previously named Day Needle) and Keeler Needle, two

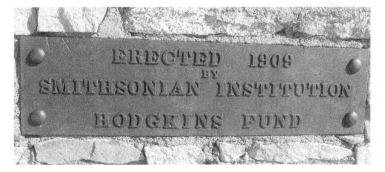

The plaque on the Smithsonian Institution research hut on the summit

14,000-foot points that are too indistinct from Mount Whitney to be considered true peaks. (Both are straightforward talus climbs from the Mount Whitney Trail, but they have vertical eastern faces.) Beyond Keeler Needle, the trail bends west for a stretch before beginning the final climb to the summit. There are a few halfhearted switchbacks up the last talus field. Nearly everyone heading down will encourage you onward with calls of, "You can't see the summit hut yet, but you're almost there." In fact, because of the summit plateau's very shallow angle, you don't see the summit hut until just minutes before you reach the top. Suddenly, the views open in every direction. See the labeled panoramic pictures on pages 136–137 to help you identify the peaks. A large summit register sits by the entrance to the stone hut. Sign your name, and then head to the giant boulders a short distance east to take a long, well-deserved break.

**HINT:** If you need to report an emergency by phone, call the Inyo County Sheriff at 760-876-5606 or, if near the summit, Sequoia National Park dispatch at 559-565-3195. A 911 call goes to the California Highway Patrol and tends to result in a delayed response.

The western slopes of Keeler Needle and Crooks Peak are simply talus piles.

Signing into the large summit register next to the hut

## STAY ON THE TRAIL

Most fatalities on Mount Whitney are due to something that doesn't, at first, seem like a very big risk: heading off trail. It is tempting for hikers to leave the trail at the snowfield on the east side of Trail Crest and glissade (slide in a controlled manner) down. Unfortunately, many who do this are inexperienced and ill-equipped. No one should ever glissade down a snowfield without an ice ax and preferably a helmet, as well as the knowledge of how to self-arrest. Even if you are carrying this equipment, be aware that this seemingly innocuous snow patch is often icy partway down and many people have lost control, sliding into the rocks below. Be smart and take the switchbacks.

*Continued on page 141*

## PANORAMIC VIEW FROM THE SUMMIT OF MOUNT WHITNEY

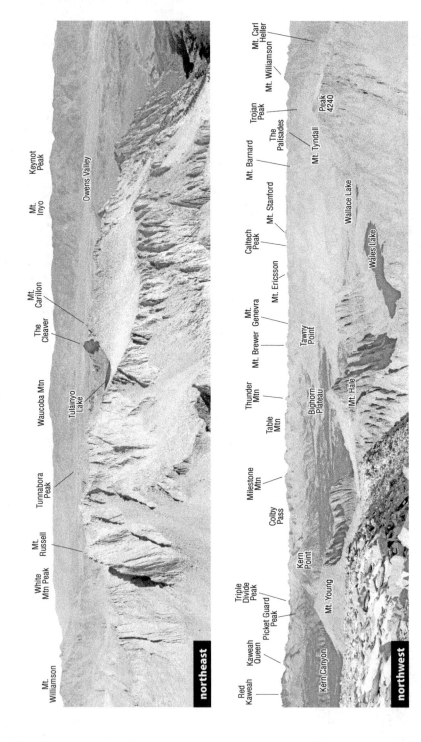

**northeast**

Mt. Williamson · White Mtn Peak · Mt. Russell · Tunnabora Peak · Waucoba Mtn · Tulainyo Lake · The Cleaver · Mt. Carillon · Mt. Inyo · Keynot Peak · Owens Valley

**northwest**

Red Kaweah · Kaweah Queen · Picket Guard Peak · Triple Divide Peak · Kern Canyon · Mt. Young · Kern Point · Colby Pass · Milestone Mtn · Table Mtn · Thunder Mtn · Bighorn Plateau · Mt. Hale · Mt. Brewer · Mt. Genevra · Tawny Point · Mt. Ericsson · Caltech Peak · Mt. Stanford · Wales Lake · Wallace Lake · Mt. Barnard · Trojan Peak · The Palisades · Mt. Tyndall · Peak 4240 · Mt. Williamson · Mt. Carl Heller

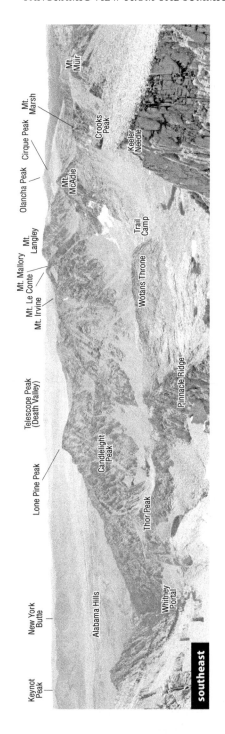

**southeast**

Keynot Peak

New York Butte

Lone Pine Peak

Telescope Peak (Death Valley)

Alabama Hills

Candlelight Peak

Thor Peak

Whitney Portal

Pinnacle Ridge

Mt. Irvine

Mt. Le Conte

Mt. Mallory

Mt. Langley

Wotans Throne

Olancha Peak

Cirque Peak

Mt. Marsh

Mt. McAdie

Trail Camp

Crooks Peak

Keeler Needle

Mt. Muir

**southwest**

Cirque Peak

Templeton Mtn

Mt. Pickering

Mt. Muir

Kern Peak

Mt. Newcomb

Joe Devel Peak

Johnson Peak

Mt. Chamberlin

Mt. Anna Mills

Coyote Peaks

Mt. Guyot

Florence Peak

Needham Mtn

Sawtooth Peak

Mt. Kaweah

Black Kaweah

Mt. Hitchcock

Hitchcock Lakes

Kern Canyon

## NAMESAKES OF WHITNEY-AREA PEAKS

Much can be learned about the history of this region by learning about the people for whom the peaks were named. Some peaks bear the names of early explorers, and many others were named for the men (yes, they were almost always men) those explorers respected. Many nearby peaks are named for astronomers, due to the spate of astronomy research on the summit around 1900. See Peter Browning's *Place Names of the Sierra Nevada* (Wilderness Press, 1991) for comprehensive information on local place names.

**Mount Whitney:** Named for Josiah Dwight Whitney, the first California state geologist. For additional information, see page 9.

**Mount Muir:** Named for John Muir, the first president of the Sierra Club, an early Sierra explorer, and an excellent natural historian. He is often considered the father of the conservation movement.

**Mount Barnard:** Named for Edward Emerson Barnard, an American astronomer in the late 1800s and early 1900s. Among his many discoveries was Jupiter's fifth moon, the last planetary satellite discovered by visual observation.

**Crooks Peak:** Named for Hulda Hoehn Crooks, a Southern California woman who climbed Mount Whitney nearly each year from age 66 to 91—from 1962 to 1987.

**Mount Hale:** Named for George Ellery Hale, an American solar astronomer in the early 1900s. His later career was spent at the California Institute of Technology (Caltech), during which time he helped found the school's Palomar Observatory in San Diego County. He passed up many invitations to participate in astronomy research atop Mount Whitney.

**Mount Carl Heller (Peak 13,211):** Unofficially named for Carl Heller, who founded the China Lake Mountain Rescue Group in 1958. His search and rescue efforts saved many lives in the Mount Whitney region.

**Mount Hitchcock:** Named for Charles Henry Hitchcock, a geology professor at Dartmouth College from 1868 to 1908.

**Mount Irvine:** Named for Andrew Irvine, who died while ascending Mount Everest in 1924.

**Keeler Needle:** Named for James Edward Keeler, an American astronomer who was director of the Lick Observatory on Mount Hamilton, east of San Jose, California. He was an assistant to astronomer Samuel Langley in 1881.

**Mount Langley:** Named for Samuel Pierpont Langley, an American astronomer who measured solar heat from near the summit of Mount Whitney in 1881.

**Mount Mallory:** Named for George Mallory, who died while ascending Mount Everest in 1924.

**Mount Marsh** (the 13,510-foot peak just southeast of Whitney Pass): Named for Gustave F. Marsh, the Lone Pine resident who built the Mount Whitney Trail and the Mount Whitney summit hut. See the book *Mount Whitney: Mountain Lore from the Whitney Store* by Doug Thompson and Elisabeth Newbold (Westwind Publishing Company, 2003) for more information.

**Mount McAdie:** Named for Alexander McAdie, a meteorologist with the San Francisco office of the U.S. Weather Bureau who took measurements atop Mount Whitney in the early 1900s.

**Mount Russell:** Named for Israel Cook Russell, an American geologist who was well known for his work around 1890 with the U.S. Geological Survey in Alaska. He was also a professor at both Columbia University and the University of Michigan.

**Mount Young:** Named for Charles Augustus Young, an American astronomer in the late 1800s and early 1900s who was a professor at Dartmouth College and later Princeton University.

Namesake peaks visible south of Mount Whitney include Mount Irvine, Mount Mallory, Mount Langley, and Mount McAdie.

## CELL PHONES AND SATELLITE COMMUNICATION ON THE SUMMIT

The expansive view from the summit of Mount Whitney includes several cell phone towers—and hikers not surprisingly often pull out their phones to report success from the summit. If this is important to you, please do so, but bear in mind that some hikers take offense to listening to long, loud phone conservations while enjoying their hard-earned alpine perch.

Cell phones, SPOT devices, and inReach satellite communicators are also all used to report injuries from the summit. This is a good thing if the injured person is unable to self-evacuate, for the two-way communication directly with the injured party gives rescuers an immediate, accurate account of the injuries, allowing them to decide on the proper course of action. However, both the wilderness rangers in Sequoia National Park and the search and rescue team in Inyo County have expressed their frustration about people calling in emergencies from the summit of Mount Whitney for relatively small injuries. Such calls often result in a helicopter evacuation for a condition that could be remedied on-site, allowing the injured person to reach the trailhead himself or with the help of a few extra people.

The rangers' frustration is manyfold: such rescues are costly and dangerous for the rescuers and take the *backcountry* out of this backcountry experience. There are extra risks associated with climbing a mountain, and people attempting to summit Mount Whitney should accept these, rather than looking at their cell phone as an emergency lifeline. Moreover, you should not decide to push your limits just because a helicopter evacuation might be possible.

Note, as well, that for most of the trail's length, there is no phone reception. When I was involved in a rescue of a man with high-altitude cerebral edema (see pages 34–39), my husband and I were unable to make a call from Trail Crest. SPOT devices and inReach satellite communicators should be able to communicate along the entire trail but are often unreliable and can give false alarms.

*Continued from page 135*

## The Descent

As you retrace your steps to Whitney Portal, keep the following in mind:

- At the junction with the John Muir Trail, the Mount Whitney Trail heads up to Trail Crest, which means you go south (left).
- You have about 300 feet of uphill on the return trip—mostly to reach Trail Crest, but there are a few other brief "ups."
- Do not take shortcuts down the often-present snowfield next to the 99 switchbacks.
- Until you are below Outpost Camp, the trail is gravelly and hard underfoot. Thrashing your feet pounding down the upper stretches of the trail is not a wise idea.
- Watch your footing on the gravel-covered granite slab between Trail Camp and a bit below Trailside Meadow.
- Stick to the trail between Trailside Meadow and Mirror Lake. If you cut down to Mirror Lake too soon, you will find yourself in increasingly steep terrain.
- Keep drinking water and eating.
- On the descent, do not leave slower party members on their own. Instead help carry their weight and encourage them along.
- Most accidents occur on the way down a mountain, when you are tired. While you want to get home and minimize hiking after dark, take it easy and take breaks. Also avoid running down the mountain—most injuries, including twisted knees and ankles, occur at the end of the day when you are tired.
- In the past 20 years, all but one fatality on the Mount Whitney Trail has been near the summit or on the descent. Pay attention to your own footing, members of your party suffering from altitude sickness, and even strangers who might need advice or assistance.

# 5 After the Hike

J ust a guess, but you may want to celebrate after your hike up Mount Whitney. The section on Lone Pine and Whitney Portal (pages 96–103) provides a list of restaurants to enjoy. If after a hearty dinner you aren't asleep and decide a dose of alcohol is in order, **Double L Bar** (226 N. Main St.) and **Jake's Saloon** (119 N. Main St.) are two options. (But avoid alcohol the day before you head up the Mount Whitney Trail; alcohol and altitude don't mix.) You will probably also want to wander along Main Street in search of some "I climbed Whitney" souvenirs. Suitable T-shirts are available in many stores.

If you have an extra day (or a few hours) before heading home, there are a handful of nearby opportunities for sightseeing that do not require much walking—a likely requirement the day after you summit.

*Opposite and above:* Looking south to the Hitchcock Lakes on the final slope to the summit

The **Museum of Western Film History,** located at 701 S. Main St., is open 10 a.m.–4 p.m. (or later on some days of the week). In addition to an informative 15-minute film recounting the history of films made in the Lone Pine region, the museum is full of props from movies filmed in the area, such as *How the West Was Won, Gunga Din,* and *Tremors.* Old Western and science fiction movies are shown some evenings for a small donation. The schedule may be on the website; otherwise stop by the museum to see what is showing. If you wish to explore the **Alabama Hills** with a bit of insider knowledge, the museum's website also has a link to an Alabama Hills Recreation Area map. See museumofwesternfilmhistory.org for more information. (The film museum also hosts the WhitneyZone webcam.)

**Manzanar National Historic Site** is a bit farther afield. This national historic site is on the location of one of the World War II Japanese war relocation camps, just off US 395, 7 miles north of Lone Pine. The visitor center is open daily in the summer, 9 a.m.–5:30 p.m. In addition to a driving loop that takes you past a few outlines of structures from the internment camp, there is a small museum and short introductory film that are worth seeing. See nps.gov/manz for more information.

# Recommended Reading

## Natural History

Beedy, Edward C., and Edward R. Pandolfino. *Birds of the Sierra Nevada: Their Natural History, Status, and Distribution.* Berkeley, CA: University of California Press, 2013.

Glazner, Allen F., and Greg M. Stock. *Geology Underfoot in Yosemite National Park.* Missoula, MT: Mountain Press Publishing Company Inc., 2010.

Jameson, E. W. Jr., and Hans J. Peeters. *Mammals of California.* Berkeley, CA: University of California Press, 2004.

Putman, Jeff, and Genny Smith, eds. *Deepest Valley: Guide to Owens Valley, Its Roadsides and Mountain Trails.* Bakersfield, CA: G. Smith Books, 1995.

Weeden, Norman F. *A Sierra Nevada Flora.* Berkeley, CA: Wilderness Press, 1996.

Wenk, Elizabeth. *Wildflowers of the High Sierra and John Muir Trail.* Birmingham, AL: Wilderness Press, 2015.

## Human History

Bowie, William. "Leveling Up Mount Whitney," *Sierra Club Bulletin* 24 (1929): 53–57.

Brewer, William Henry, and William H. Alsup. *Such a Landscape!: A Narrative of the 1864 California Geological Survey Exploration of Yosemite, Sequoia & Kings Canyon from the Diary, Field Notes, Letters & Reports of William Henry Brewer.* El Portal, CA: Yosemite Association, 1999.

Browning, Peter. *Place Names of the Sierra Nevada: From Abbot to Zumwalt.* Berkeley, CA: Wilderness Press, 1991.

Dyer, Hubert. "The Mt. Whitney Trail," *Sierra Club Bulletin* 1 (1893): 1–8.

Farquhar, Francis P. "The Story of Mount Whitney," *Sierra Club Bulletin* 14 (1929): 39–53.

———. *History of the Sierra Nevada.* Berkeley, CA: University of California Press, 1965.

King, Clarence. *Mountaineering in the Sierra Nevada.* Lincoln, NE: University of Nebraska Press, 1997.

Le Conte, J. N. "Notes on the King's River and Mt. Whitney Trails (July and August, 1890)," *Sierra Club Bulletin* 1 (1894): 93–106.

Moore, James G. *Exploring the Highest Sierra.* Stanford, CA: Stanford University Press, 2000.

Parsons, Marion R. "With the Sierra Club in the Kern Cañon," *Sierra Club Bulletin* 7 (1909): 23–32.

Thompson, Doug, and Elisabeth Newbold. *Mount Whitney: Mountain Lore from the Whitney Store.* El Cajon, CA: Westwind Publishing Company, 2003.

## History of Astronomy Research on Mount Whitney

McAdie, Alexander G. "Mount Whitney as a Site for a Meteorological Observatory," *Sierra Club Bulletin* 5 (1904): 87–101.

Osterbrock, Donald E. "To Climb the Highest Mountain: W. W. Campbell's 1909 Mars Expedition to Mount Whitney," *Journal of Historical Astronomy* 20 (1989): 77–97.

## Precautions and Considerations

Aksamit, Inga, and Kenny Meyer. "Altitude Acclimatization." facebook.com/groups/789714584455856.

Hackett, Peter H., and Robert C. Roach. "High-Altitude Illness," *New England Journal of Medicine* 345 (2001): 107–114.

Houston, Charles, et al. *Going Higher: Oxygen, Man, and Mountains.* Seattle, WA: Mountaineers Books, 2005.

Wagner, Dale R., et al. "Variables Contributing to Acute Mountain Sickness on the Summit of Mt Whitney," *Wilderness & Environmental Medicine* 17 (2006): 221–228.

"The WhitneyZone." *Mt. Whitney Hikers Association.* whitneyzone.com.

# Index

photographed by Douglas Bock

## About the Author

Since childhood, Lizzy Wenk has hiked and climbed in the Sierra Nevada with her family. After she started college, she found excuses to spend every summer in the Sierra, with its beguiling landscape, abundant flowers, and near-perfect weather. During those summers, she worked as a research assistant for others and completed her own Ph.D. thesis research on the effects of rock type on alpine plant distribution and physiology. But much of the time, she hikes simply for leisure. Obsessively wanting to explore every bit of the Sierra, she has hiked thousands of on- and off-trail miles and climbed more than 500 peaks in the mountain range. She is especially fond of the steep, rugged peaks in the Whitney region, and she visits the area to hike and climb each year. Lizzy, husband Douglas, and daughters Eleanor and Sophia currently live in Sydney, Australia, but continue to consider the Eastern Sierra home and return to the mountains each summer.